"What a terrific book, and what a great contribution. All of us who teach courses on the history of medicine or on the intersections among religion, health, and healing owe a great debt of gratitude to Gillian McCann. This is a book that I've been waiting for—and praying for—for many years. It should become a go-to text for such courses for years to come".

**Jeff Levin, PhD, MPH,**
*University Professor of Epidemiology and Population Health and professor of medical humanities at Baylor University*

"Gillian McCann has written a marvelous book that helps us to better understand the world's religions through the lens of health and healing. What is particularly impressive is how she covers both the different traditions as well as how those traditions have changed over time".

**Amir Hussain,**
*professor of theological studies, Loyola Marymount University, Los Angeles*

"The book is skilfully written for clients and healthcare providers by a qualified professional. It is a courageous book that holds transformational potential for clients and caregivers to see into the varied meanings within the experience of illness, a relationality that enhances one's well-being, and a peace beyond the suffering".

**Rev. Mary Sue Barnett,**
*level 1 trauma center chaplain and co-editor of Spiritual Healing from Sexual Violence: An Intersectional Guide*

# Health and Healing in World Religions

*Health and Healing in World Religions* is a comprehensive introduction to the field that explores the research that links spirituality and well-being, including work with addiction and trauma.

Each chapter includes an introduction to and summary of each tradition, questions at the conclusion, and boxes that highlight key ideas from the chapter using an example and interviews with medical professionals and other healers. *Health and Healing in World Religions* looks at cutting edge interfaces between spirituality and health such as mindfulness practices, addiction programmes, indigenous approaches to healing, traditional Chinese medicine, yoga and Ayurveda, and more. The text provides an overview of the research and practice all in one place and includes extensive bibliographies and resource guides for ease of reference.

*Health and Healing in World Religions* is derived from over 20 years of teaching and research in health and healing and comes from an in-depth understanding of religion and spirituality. It is a vital guide to understanding cultural competency in the healing professions and the need to understand the cultural and spiritual traditions of clients.

**Gillian McCann** is an associate professor in the Religions and Cultures Program at Nipissing University in Ontario, Canada.

# Health and Healing in World Religions

*A Guide to Developing Cultural Competencies*

GILLIAN MCCANN

Routledge
Taylor & Francis Group
NEW YORK AND LONDON

Designed cover image: © LaylaBird Getty Images

First published 2025
by Routledge
605 Third Avenue, New York, NY 10158

and by Routledge
4 Park Square, Milton Park, Abingdon, Oxon, OX14 4RN

*Routledge is an imprint of the Taylor & Francis Group, an informa business*



*Library of Congress Cataloging-in-Publication Data*
Names: McCann, Gillian, 1965- author.
Title: Health and healing in world religions : a guide to developing cultural competencies / Gillian McCann.
Description: New York, NY : Routledge, 2025. | Includes bibliographical references and index. |
Identifiers: LCCN 2024028469 (print) | LCCN 2024028470 (ebook) | ISBN 9781032739243 (hbk) | ISBN 9781032739236 (pbk) | ISBN 9781003471769 (ebk)
Subjects: LCSH: Healing--Religious aspects. | Spiritual healing. | Cultural competence.
Classification: LCC BL65.M4 M395 2025 (print) | LCC BL65.M4 (ebook) | DDC 201/.661--dc23/eng/20240905
LC record available at https://lccn.loc.gov/2024028469
LC ebook record available at https://lccn.loc.gov/2024028470

ISBN: 978-1-032-73924-3 (hbk)
ISBN: 978-1-032-73923-6 (pbk)
ISBN: 978-1-003-47176-9 (ebk)

DOI: 10.4324/9781003471769

Typeset in Times New Roman
by SPi Technologies India Pvt Ltd (Straive)

This work was written on the traditional territory of the Nbisiing Anishinaabeg people and, specifically, the Nipissing First Nation, within lands protected by the Robinson Huron Treaty of 1850. I am grateful to live and learn on these lands with all our relations.

This book is dedicated with gratitude to the late Dr David Kinsley and all the healers who work selflessly every day for the well-being of the world.

# Contents

# Acknowledgement

I would like to thank Anna Moore, Publisher, Sophie Dracott, Editorial Assistant, the team at Routledge, and the anonymous reviewers for their help in bringing this book to publication. I would also like to thank Gitte Bechsgaard and Angela Rogers for their support and interest throughout the years of writing.

# Preface

Year after year when teaching the first class of the course Health, Healing and Religion I consistently look out onto a sea of mystified and shocked faces. Sometimes there are crossed arms and sceptical expressions. For many people the assumption is that being religious can only correlate to poorer health and the idea that religion can contribute to better health is almost inconceivable. There is vague notion that certain traditions are opposed to medical intervention or are "fatalistic". Images of television faith healers tend to dance in their heads and various stereotypes about religion generally.

I first began teaching on the topic of health and religion at McMaster University in Hamilton, Ontario over 20 years ago. The McMaster course had been developed by Dr David Kinsley who also wrote one of the first books on the topic. It was further developed by medical anthropologist Dr Donna L. Seamone. Sadly, Dr Kinsley had passed away by the time I was teaching the course but I have been greatly inspired by his work in my own writing and teaching.

Since the publication of Kinsley's *Health, Healing and Religion* in 1995 a growing body of evidence reveals that religious and spiritual people tend to be healthier both mentally and physically. This research also has made explicit the world's religious traditions' direct connection with healing. However, the general lack of awareness of this connection reveals that this information is not making its way into the awareness of the broader public. This work is meant to begin to address this gap in knowledge.

In teaching on the topic of health, healing and religion I have come into contact with those, often in the field of health care, interested in the long-neglected role of spiritual and religious in healing. Working as they do in the trenches these nurses, paramedics, psychologists, chaplains, and social workers have had to face the hardest and deepest questions of meaning in working with their clients.

In helping people and their families heal, or accompanying them through the process of death and dying, many have felt their own lack of training and competency in this area.

I have also been surprised, over the years, at how little guidance health care workers are given in the area of philosophy and spirituality. One young nurse in training recounted her first experience of the death of a patient and not knowing how to react—either in terms of her own emotions or those of the bereaved family. While medical training is excellent at giving technical instruction there is often little guidance given regarding the more human side of health for both the patients and those attending them.

It is precisely because health and healing move us into the realm of human embodiment and mortality that philosophical and religious questions cannot be ignored. Facing illness often provokes an existential crisis for individuals, their families, and communities. It may be the first time that a person is confronted directly with their own mortality. In our death denying society this often comes as a profound shock. As Raymond (1982) argues, biomedicine partakes of religion because it operates within the field of "ultimate concern" and must draw on religious and philosophical ideas regarding a well lived life (p. 213).

Due to the vast amount of available material on the topic, I have had to pick and choose from the many examples of the connections between religion and health and healing. As a result, I have chosen certain traditions to highlight key principles. This does not mean they don't exist in other religious and spiritual traditions. Phenomenon such as catharsis, use of sacred narrative, the figure of the wounded healer, confession, social support, and therapeutic alliance, ideas of healing vocation exist across cultures and traditions. This fact speaks to enduring aspects of the human psyche and to what allows human beings to maintain mental, emotional, physical, and spiritual health.

I also recognize that healing systems and religions are not static and they change and evolve. Religions and cultures have always created complex syncretisms within a variety of encounters including: colonization, movement of populations, and in the contemporary period via a variety of media. When looking at practices like Ayurveda and Unani, there is a recognition that as they developed they also came into an often challenging relationship with colonialism and what has been referred to as medical imperialism.

The contemporary period has witnessed the movement of these systems outside their places of origin and the process of development continues in countries like Canada and the United States. Systems such as Ayurveda and Traditional Chinese Medicine (TCM), while part of primary healthcare in their countries of origin, have had to negotiate a more problematic terrain and have been styled as "alternative medicine" in countries like Canada and the United States.

This book is written from the standpoint of cultural, religious, and medical pluralism. The historical record reveals clearly that those working in the fields of healing always shared information and worked across culture and religion. This medical cosmopolitanism was based on a desire to heal and to use whatever was efficacious regardless of its origins.

Refusing to engage with other worldviews can render non-allopathic systems of healing unintelligible. Just as we affirm the integrity of the world's religions, we also need to recognize their healing systems and approaches to health and well-being. This is not a standpoint of mere tolerance but recognition that there is much to learn from these sources of wisdom.

The often sterile debates held around secularization and religion tend to focus on religious belief. While these are, of course, important this obscures how religions actually work. The world's religious traditions are systems and life-ways meant to allow for human flourishing both individually and in a community. These traditions also contain profound modalities that can contribute to resilience and recovery in the face of the challenges and suffering that are part of human life.

Most of the spiritual traditions examined in this work understand health and healing within the larger context of social well-being, aesthetics, relationships with the natural world, and broader concepts of a well lived life. If the reader is fixated only on principles derived from biomedicine, that keeps all these dimensions separate and insists only on those proved by double blind studies, again the wisdom of these approaches recedes and becomes difficult to discern.

In some cases the inability to perceive the whole healing system has resulted in distortions as a result of attempting to shoe horn them into scientific categories. There has also been a tendency to try to cherry pick aspects of these complex systems in our constant search for a magic bullet cure-all. This can become a kind of faddish trumpeting of wonder drugs such as turmeric or gingko using their origins merely as exotic trappings.

For ease of reading these traditions are presented as separate when in lived reality they often overlap or have been historically influenced by one another. A woman in a North American city who is struggling with infertility may go to a practitioner of TCM, a naturopath, attend yoga classes, and see a medical doctor. Human beings are extremely pragmatic when it comes to health care and will seek out whatever treatment is effective.

A holistic approach is the connecting thread that runs through these varied traditions. The insistence on viewing a person within the tapestry of their whole life is clearly one of the reasons why these forms have survived for millennia. Another reason for the popularity of these approaches is the desire for a more human and warm relationship between the patient and practitioner. It is clear that people are voting with their feet as over 50% of people in the United States and Canada report that they have consulted some form of alternative health and healing.

As the health budgets of countries around the world balloon and take up increasing amounts of their nation's Gross Domestic Product (GDP), openness to these approaches has become crucially important. The problem of life-style illnesses have now moved beyond countries like Canada and the US and are having an impact all around the globe. A growing recognition of the resources offered by religious and spiritual traditions are now being recognized by governments. One example is the National Health Service in the United Kingdom which now covers the cost of non-allopathic approaches such as training in meditative practices. Mindfulness courses are now offered all over the world and are often recommended by psychologists and counselors.

While studies and research are included throughout this monograph, I am proposing that these systems be recognized as having their own ontologies and epistemologies. The work also engages with the struggles of various medical systems in "articulating medical authority" often in a sceptical and challenging environment (Alavi, 2008, p. 5).

Because this work is as an overview I am making no claims for completeness. Each of these traditions are complex and diverse, often with many different branches and denominations and have experienced complex developments over time. It is humanly impossible to have expertise in all these fields. As a result, the bibliographies are meant as jumping off points for further research and reflection. The synopsis of the tradition at the beginning and the end of each chapter is meant to help orient the reader to the basic beliefs and practices of each of the religions.

I am aware that another person would write a completely different book. *Health and Healing in World Religions* reflects my journey and experiences so far in relationship with my students and the community in which I live. I have been deeply influenced and healed by practitioners from many of the world's traditions. It is my hope that this work will contribute to the ability of more people to benefit from these varied healing systems.

These resources can be made available both to clients and also for those who work in the caring professions that have notoriously high rates of burnout. Nurses, doctors, social workers, psychologists, and chaplains often work with people at their most challenging moments. These professions/vocations ask a great deal of those who practice them. Spiritual and religious traditions offer a wide array of practices that can contribute to the well-being of those working in healthcare.

Exercises and questions are included at the end of each chapter. These have been work-shopped in many of my classes over the years. An example is a student of mine who was in a social work programme who worked on the four directions exercise. This reflection on well-being in the sectors of mind, emotions, body, spirit resulted in her exclaiming, "I am terrible in all of them!" We all appreciated her honesty and humour and, of course, this awareness provides a great deal of useful information.

Without this kind of periodic self-reflection it can become very easy to simply soldier on not paying attention. This, in turn, often leads to a cascade of physical, mental, and emotional effects that can ultimately lead to burnout This is particularly the case for health professionals and those who work in the caring professions, who often ignore their own well-being, in their focus on caring for others.

Bringing religious and spiritual traditions back into the conversation has important implications for health care systems and the health care curriculum. Figuring out how to facilitate the interface between these traditions and secular institutions has already begun in many forms from university to curricula to health care practice. However, challenges remain in accelerating this process.

Engaging with moral and philosophical systems also leads to the subject of healing at the societal level. The fact that certain people and communities have a much-reduced life expectancy in wealthy countries like Canada and the US points to issues that go far beyond the consulting room. Religious traditions have had a great deal to say about what we owe our neighbours and the impossibility of indifference.

With this work I hope to make a contribution to imagining how health care workers and systems can draw on the powerful resources that exist within these traditions. Moving away from the Cartesian split that has typified western health care for centuries is vital. Only this will allow all of us to benefit, both personally and as communities, from the insights of these traditions. Engaging with the whole person will allow religion and science to come back into dialogue.

## REFERENCES

Alavi, Seema (2008). *Islam and Healing. Loss and Recovery of an Indo-Muslim Medical Tradition. 1600–1900*. Palgrave Macmillan.

Raymond, Janice G. (1982). Medicine as Patriarchal Religion. *Journal of Medicine and Philosophy*. 7 (2), 197–216.

## FURTHER READING

Apoorva Rama, *Policy Research Perspectives National Health Expenditures, 2019: Steady Spending Growth Despite Increases in Personal Health Care Expenditures in Advance of the Pandemic*. American Medical Association, https://www.ama-assn.org/system/files/2021-05/prp-annual-spending-2019.pdf

Fatma Al-Maskari, *Lifestyle Diseases: An Economic Burden on the Health Services*. UN Chronicle, https://www.un.org/en/chronicle/article/lifestyle-diseases-economic-burden-health-services

*National Health Expenditure Trends*, Canadian Institute for Health Information, November 4, 2021, https://www.cihi.ca/en/national-health-expenditure-trends

Pew Research Center (February 2, 2017). Americans' Healthcare Behaviors and Use of Conventional and Alternative Medicine. https://www.pewresearch.org/science/2017/02/02/americans-health-care-behaviors-and-use-of-conventional-and-alternative-medicine/

# 1 What is Health: Understanding the Connection Between Religion, Spirituality and Well-being

If asked directly most people would likely assume that religion can only have a negative impact on health. However, there is a growing body of research that reveals an intimate connection as supported by recent findings in *JAMA*. The carefully researched study led by Harvard Medical School faculty recommends that, "health care professionals recognize and consider the benefits of spiritual community as part of efforts to improve wellbeing" (Balboni et al., 2022, p.195).

Understanding why so few understand the connection between religion and health requires looking at how we conceptualize religion and health. What is meant by the word health? Are we simply referring to an absence of disease or malfunction or is it something more expansive? And what do our ideas about health say about our understanding of the human body and the larger context of health and well-being?

From a strictly physicalist understanding of health and healing religion and spirituality are seen as contaminating a purely secular field of concern. With the ascension of the scientific and technological world view, we find a split that has characterized western culture from at least the beginning of the 18th century.

The metaphor of the machine is generally the one used to imagine both society and the human body. All challenges were now to be

DOI: 10.4324/9781003471769-1

faced and resolved through rational planning and technological skill. From within this worldview spirituality of any kind was understood as an archaic remnant of the past characterized by superstition and irrationality and something that should be excluded from the public sphere.

Because a materialist paradigm is held by so many people in western society, whether they are conscious of it or not, many view their body much like a car. Although, in truth, many people treat their vehicles better than their bodies. This very common metaphor of body as machine has a cascade of impacts relating to how we treat both our bodies and that of others.

The current common sense understanding of health is one of a body free of serious impairment, in good working order, and autonomous. Increasingly, the body is seen as a "vehicle to be controlled and manipulated" and as "a production/consumption machine" (Dissanayake, 1993, p. 32). This view of health also removes it from the larger context of community and the natural environment.

In order to engage meaningfully with other ways of understanding health and healing it is vital to move beyond the idea that there is only one way to understand it. Coward and Ratanakul (1999) argue that to insist on only one view of health is to engage in biomedical imperialism (p. 5). In fact, colonial systems have routinely attempted to reconfigure the medical systems of the territories that they control.

It has been argued that the physicalist approach to medicine, that focuses only the mechanics of the human body, is a cultural system unto itself. In fact, seen from this perspective, almost everyone, regardless of their cultural or religious background, feels a profound state of alienation and disorientation when entering into a hospital or other institutionalized healthcare environment. This is true for physicians themselves when they find themselves patients within the healthcare system.

Hahn (1995) writes that the sudden shift from highly competent physician to, "a fearful patient, threatened by a possibly deadly disease". can be profoundly disorienting (p. 234). Doctors who have written about their experiences often evince shock at the immediately depersonalizing and alienating nature of entering into the medical system. These experiences of fear and a sense of vulnerability often transform the physicians' attitudes both towards their work and their patients.

Moving into the world of contemporary health care we find ourselves in a foreign land with its own arcane language, strict forms of hierarchy, hygiene and strange machinery. The person who enters into a healthcare setting is also routinely stripped of their regular clothing and identity. This feeling of being in a foreign land is common to most people's experience of biomedicine with its focus on technology, efficiency, and testing. From this point of view the contemporary hospital is a "highly sophisticated technocratic factory, the more technology the hospital has to offer, the better it is considered to be" (p. 150).

The paradigm of the body as machine often results in doctor's appointments that consist mostly in referral for tests. From the point of view of most of the world's religious traditions biomedicine is the outlier here. Most emphasize the "relational self" which is understood as being an open, porous system in relationship with healer, community, ancestors, land, and the divine. From within this worldview the relationship between healer and client is of central importance.

World view also profoundly impacts attitudes towards end-of-life care or attitudes towards a body that cannot be "fixed" as in the case of chronic illnesses. Death, from a purely biomedical point of view, is often seen as a failure. The rise of the palliative care and hospice movements have been one of the spaces in which more holistic and spiritually based approaches have been able to re-enter the medical system.

The importance of understanding religious views of health and healing includes recognizing it as part of the comprehensive worldview that shapes ideas about the meaning and end of life, ethics, relationships, the environment, and the human body. Religious traditions also address themselves to the challenges of life which include chronic illness and the aging process.

At the same time as the mechanistic paradigm seems to grow stronger, study after study is revealing that religious people are healthier overall both mentally and physically. Beginning in the 1970's researchers in the western world began to look at why this might be the case. Since then, a vast body of research has emerged studying the benefits of practices like meditation, yoga, ritual, and community worship.

Work in the field of trauma research and affective immunology has demonstrated clearly that healing needs to take into account the entire human system and shows clearly the connection between mind and body. These new insights help to explain why syndromes such as addiction, have often proven to be so intractable to biomedical interventions.

This research reveals the ways in which religious and spiritual traditions reject the Cartesian split between mind and body. The idea that the human body and idea of health can be abstracted from context is increasingly untenable. As Van Der Kolk (2014) notes succinctly, "your zip code even more than your genetic code, determines whether you will lead a safe and healthy life" (p. 350).

The ongoing research into the connection between religion, spirituality and health also has implication for the standard curriculum for medical doctors, nurses, social workers, and psychologists. The United States has been at the forefront of these efforts due to the work of groups such as the George Washington Institute of Spirituality and Health. Now between 75 and 90% of medical schools in the United Sates offer courses on health, healing, and religion.

Although many Canadian universities offer courses on the topic at the undergraduate level, at the institutional level Canadian institutions have been much more resistant to engaging systematically with these findings and including them in medical training and curriculum. As a result, according to Tsz et al (2023) "many physicians express discomfort and inadequate knowledge around addressing patients' spirituality, which results in more aggressive treatments, poor quality of life, and reduced patient satisfaction" (p. 105).

In order to begin to understand why so many struggle to recognize a beneficial connection between religion and health we need first to look at these two terms. While a definition of both the words religion and health may seem straight forward attempts at definition quickly reveal that they are not and move us into culturally influenced ideas and philosophies that take in entire worldviews.

## WHAT IS RELIGION?

As anyone who works in the field of religious studies knows the quickest way to start an argument is to ask the above question. It is important to note there is no one accepted definition in the field. Instead, most scholars use working definitions that fit with their approach to the topic. The difficulty of finding one accepted definition points to the complexity of the phenomenon.

One definition of religion that seemed very promising when first introduced by Protestant theologian Paul Tillich (1957) was the idea that religion related to "ultimate concern" for a person (p. 1). This definition is useful due to its breadth and can be applied to many, if not all, religions and spiritualties. However, it's capaciousness is also its weakness and many have pointed out that a hockey card collection might be someone's ultimate concern—is it then a religion?

In searching for a concise explanation of religion that is also capacious enough here are two other definitions that can be helpful in providing orientation. *The Encyclopedia of Religion* (1987) defines religion as:

> the organization of life around the depth dimensions of experience-varied in form, completeness, and clarity in accordance with the environing culture.
>
> *(p. 7)*

This definition offers a more detailed description and includes within it the idea of culture. It also points to the concept of a transcendent dimension to life beyond the five senses.

One of the most influential definitions of the word religion was proposed by Émile Durkheim, (1912/1995) One of the founders of the field sociology he defined religion as:

> A unified system of beliefs and practices relative to sacred things that is to say, things set apart and forbidden—beliefs and practices which unite in one simple moral community called church, all those who adhere to it.
>
> *(p. 44)*

As a sociologist, Durkheim was principally interested in the social dimensions of religion. His work emerged in the context of a rapidly secularizing society in France in the early 20th century. Durkheim was concerned that the lessening power of religion would lead to loosening of community bonds and have negative impacts on individuals such as states moral disorientation.

In work spear headed by the George Washington Institute for Spirituality & Health, the concept of spirituality, rather than the term religion, has been advocated for use in the larger sphere of health care. Spirituality is defined as:

> the aspect of humanity that refers to the way individuals seek and express meaning and purpose, and the way they experience their connectedness to the moment, to self, to others to nature and to the significant and sacred.
>
> *(Puchalski and Ferrell, 2010, p. 25)*

This definition is clearly much broader and meant to work in a variety of multicultural healthcare settings from palliative and hospice care to the emergency room.

Any useful working definition related to health and healing recognizes the many dimensions of religion including: attitudes towards the body, material practice, world view, creation of community and practices that support resilience. This understanding takes into account more than simply the belief in a transcendent dimension but also the day-to-day practices such as prayer and meditation and narratives that offer a sacralized world view, and ceremonies and rituals that draw communities together.

Buddhist scholar Trevor Ling presents a vital corrective to a common misperception that religion is a strictly individual matter. Rather than being only a "personal system of consolation", according to Ling (1973) religions are, in fact, representative of whole civilizations and therefore represent a whole worldview, and a "total prescription for the ordering of human affairs" (p. 26).

The field of the material culture of religion has offered an important corrective regarding how religion is understood. Morgan (2010) argues that religion exists within a "felt life" and is a deeply embodied practice. Religion, from this point of view, is bound up in sacred space, family dinners, and habits of charity. Describing pilgrims on the Compostella de Santiago, he notes that the experience included the sounds of the crowds, the flickering light in the churches and the smell of, "sweaty bodies, baked bread and incense" (p. 8).

It is only when viewed in this multifaceted way that the interface between spirituality and health and healing can be properly understood. Because it is the impact of all these aspects, as a holistic system, that contributes to well-being. The way that religious world views shape ideas about the human body, the role of community and relationship are all vital aspects of what contributes to better health.

## DEFINITIONS OF HEALTH

The word health is another term that seems commonsensical but, in fact, is shaped by culture, time period and worldview. In fact, all ideas of health are socially constructed rather than universal. It is also important to recognize that traditions conceive of the human person and their place within the world and cosmos will radically impact their ideas about health and healing. As Ross (2014) writes, "different definitions of a healthy person will require different healing approaches" (p. 232).

A useful place to start when defining the word health is with the definition used by the World Health Organization (WHO). The preamble to their Constitution, originally written in 1946, and updated since, states:

> Health is a state of complete physical, mental and social well-being and not merely the absence of disease or infirmity. The enjoyment of the highest attainable standard of health is one of the fundamental rights of every human being without distinction of race, religion, political belief, economic or social condition.
>
> *(World Health Organization (WHO), 2023)*

This definition offers a more nuanced conception of health that moves beyond the idea of fixing an injury or recovery from illness. Health is understood as a dynamic process related to resilience and a "resource for living".

The WHO definition clearly recognizes the social context of health and healing and impact of mental, societal, and economic factors on health and well-being. This definition emphasizes the role of governments in ensuring good health, the necessity of justice and redistribution of wealth and resources and the vital role of public health policy.

Many of the health professions have accepted the WHO definition but have curiously given little real attention to the question of the meaning of the word health. Likely due to its practical nature, the nursing profession has been slow to grapple with the question of what is meant by health.

In a 2015 article in the *International Journal of Nursing Knowledge* written by Ahmad et al. it is noted that while health is a central concept it is not clearly defined in nursing and other disciplines. The authors suggest that, "Additional concept development and clarification is needed. Health should be defined in a consistent manner in order to help nurses and other healthcare professionals provide healthcare services and interventions" (p. 5).

The rather hazy notion of what is meant by the word health is no doubt related to the crisis-focused nature of our physical and mental healthcare systems. When addressing issues of acuity there is no question that the biomedical system is effective and life saving. However, when looking at the domains of preventative medicine or facilitating human flourishing there has been little attention given to the larger meaning of health.

The roots of the word health itself are instructive as they link back to the idea of wholeness in the Old English root *hal*. As Fields

(2002) notes English words such as health and therapy contain within them ideas about restoring to wholeness, cleansing, and purification (p. 3). This in turn connects to worldviews that connected mind, body, and spirit. Health, then, is far more than simply an absence of debilitating symptoms.

It is clear that there are many ways of understanding the word health. Even the most mechanistically oriented practitioner generally has a sense that full health includes more than simply recovery from a broken arm or high fever. Health is intuitively felt to include full energy, not just to face life's ongoing challenges, but also to allow for social life, creativity, and contribution to society.

## DIMENSIONS OF HEALING: THE CONNECTIONS BETWEEN RELIGION, SPIRITUALITY AND HEALTH

Even a cursory look at world religions shows the integral connection between religion, health, and healing. Both Jesus and the Buddha were understood as being healers in the broadest sense and the New Testament is full of descriptions of Jesus healing both physical and mental afflictions. In the Muslim tradition Allah is referred to as *Al-Shafi* (The Great Healer) and the alleviation of pain and suffering is considered to be a *sine qua non* of moral action. Buddhist and Christian monks and nuns have been among the world's great herbalists and healers and were often the first to keep medical records and pharmacopoeia.

Healing systems such as Ayurveda developed directly from the religious scripture of Hinduism and Chinese traditions, particularly Daoism directly influenced the healing system of Traditional Chinese Medicine (TCM). In the case of Indigenous spirituality, health cannot be removed from the larger concept of a well-lived life in relationship to human beings, non-human living beings, and the land.

Jeff Levin, one of the pioneers in the field of health, healing, and religion began to make the connection as a graduate student. While researching he noticed that many of the health surveys conducted by the National Institutes of Health in the United States included questions regarding religion. As a result, information related to the connection between religion and health was available but hadn't been collected and interpreted. In looking at the evidence, Levin (2001) states, "there is scarcely a disease that has not been studied in relation to religion and moreover findings are remarkably consistent" (p. 6).

This research, however, has largely failed to reach mainstream discourse. Contributing to the inability to see the connection between religion and health, is the fact that often the body is considered to be an objective fact.

While in secular western culture the body has been radically stripped of all meaning, most of the world's religious traditions maintain a more compassionate and caring view of human embodiment. The body is generally understood as partaking of the sacred so there are injunctions against harming both one's own body and the body of others.

In discussing the social construction of medical knowledge, Freund and McGuire (1999) have characterized biomedical ideology as consisting in: mind-body dualism, physical reductionism, specific etiology, the machine metaphor and regimen and control (pp. 212–214). This way of understanding both the human body and health, have become so ubiquitous that for some people it is almost impossible to understand that any other paradigm is possible.

However, even the most strictly scientific doctor recognizes that alongside treatment it is the body and more intangible sources of healing that are necessary for treatment to be successful. These may include the natural healing forces found in nature and the personal will of the patient to recover. Also, many healthcare practitioners belong to faith traditions themselves and may view their work as a vocation and service.

The reason for the connection between health, healing, and religion can be quickly understood when considering the fact that nearly every religion espouses beliefs that govern and regulate behaviour. The body is a primary site of concern for most of the world's spiritual traditions. For example, the Muslim tradition forbids the drinking of alcohol as do some sects of Christianity, the Buddhist tradition warns against the use of intoxicants of any kind whether it be drugs or alcohol and Jains forbid the consumption of meat.

While few will argue that that every member of these traditions maintain these injunctions to the letter, they do set clear limits on potentially damaging behaviours. Religious traditions also surround the acts of eating and drinking with a framework of meaning. These beliefs and practices tend to encourage a healthier and more social approach towards diet enfolding it within a larger ethical framework.

Another key component that contributes to both physical and mental health is the importance of community. Buddhism cites the *sangha* (Buddhist community) as one of the three jewels that is at the heart of the practice of the tradition. In Judaism and Christianity congregational worship and community service is emphasized while in Islam the concept of the *ummah* (the transnational community) is a pillar of the religion. Most religious traditions also have strong sanctions against harming one's own body or the body of others.

Religious and spiritual traditions have always understood that a sense of meaning and purpose and life in a community is vital to human well-being. Religion has traditionally played a vital role in protection against states of *anomie*, a feeling of social dislocation and alienation. Work done by Esfahani-Smith reveals that, in fact, meaning is a much more important concept than happiness for the well-being of both individuals and society.

The larger architecture of religious traditions such as retreats, pilgrimage and days of rest and celebrations also all contribute to overall health and well-being These practices emphasize the need to take time for self-reflection and rest and to focus on higher values and on friends and family alongside concerns about career and work.

The world's spiritual traditions offer prayers for those who are ill and many enjoin their members to show compassion for those who are suffering. This may include calls to visit the sick, to support care-givers, to financially endow healing institutions and places of education.

Research is now demonstrating that practices of meditation, contemplation, ritual, and ceremony are calming to the nervous system. From the drumming used in Indigenous traditions to the rosaries of Christianity and malas and prayer beads of Hinduism and Islam, all these practices show real effects on the ability to maintain mental equilibrium and calm the body and mind.

There is also an increased openness to looking at the connections between religion, spirituality, and psychological well-being. Froma Walsh (2009), clinical psychologist and academic, states:

> Over the centuries people have lit candles, prayed together, meditated, and quietly turned to faith for solace, strength and connectedness in their lives. In times of crisis and adversity, spiritual beliefs and practices have fostered resilience and recovery from loss, trauma, and suffering.
>
> *(p. 3)*

This idea that religious and spiritual traditions can aid in resilience is slowly beginning to be engaged with from within the world of psychology and psychotherapy.

In the field of adolescent psychology research clearly demonstrates the positive contribution of religion and spirituality. Clinical psychologist and researcher Lisa Miller (2016) has demonstrated that spiritual development in adolescents has demonstrable protective benefits. Miller writes that health spirituality can mitigate:

> the most serious health challenges of adolescence such as risk taking, depression, substance abuse, and severe affective disorders. Spirituality is also strongly associated with positive inner aspects, such as meaning, purpose and optimism.
>
> *(p. 17)*

While initially greeted with some hostility, Miller's work is getting increased traction as witnessed by her best-selling book *The Spiritual Child* (2016).

James L. Griffith (2012) has suggested ways for mental health professionals to use religion and spirituality as resource in their practice. He emphasizes that there are concrete ways in which to ensure this is done respectfully giving the FICA interviewing tool as an example (p. 227). This tool of assessment does not require that the practitioner has the same beliefs as the client. Griffith also offers guidelines for determining if religion is healthy expression or emerging from psychopathology. He notes that healthy forms of religiosity "stimulate creativity, personal growth, and a deepening compassion for others" (p. 231).

## *FICA Interviewing Tool*

- F—Faith and belief—Do you consider yourself to be spiritual or religious? Do you have spiritual beliefs that help you cope with stress?
- I—Importance—What importance does your faith or belief have in your life?
- C—Community—Are you part of a spiritual or religious community?
- A—Address in care—How would you like me, your healthcare provider, to address these issues in your healthcare?

(Griffith,2012, p. 227)

Increasingly, healthcare professionals themselves have begun to question the downstream approach that focuses solely on symptoms and their management. In his TED talk Rishi Manchanda, MD notes that the health of his patients is impacted by their living conditions in general and this is linked to growing inequities in the distribution of wealth. Health, from this point of view cannot simply be an individual concern—it is linked to the larger community and political decisions that determine access, housing, green space, and nutritious food.

Studies of the blue zones of the world where people live healthily into old age have demonstrated that good health is fostered within a tapestry of practices. In *The Village Effect* (2014) social psychologist Susan Pinker has demonstrated that longevity may have as much to do with strong caring, social networks including family, and both secular and religious communities as with any other factor.

Sociologist Peggy Thoits (2011) has demonstrated the bulwark that religion can provide in her idea of the buffering hypothesis. This buffering effect is the result of religious belief and practice that contribute to resilience (pp. 145–161). Religions provide this in a wide variety of ways from providing philosophical solace to concrete support and protection.

As the connections between religion and spirituality and well-being come into clearer focus those who work in health care are beginning to grapple with the idea of culturally competent/congruent care. Wehbe-Alamah et al. (2020) note that while literature on the topic remains sparse awareness of the beliefs of clients, "assists nurses and other healthcare providers in the delivery of culturally competent care" (p. 119).

Desire for more holistic approaches to care have resulted in many people in the western world seeking out alternative forms of healing ranging from massage to Reiki, to Traditional Chinese Medicine (TCM), and Ayurveda in unprecedented numbers. Countries like India, China, and Thailand continue to support their Indigenous forms of healing alongside western biomedicine. Indigenous communities are reclaiming their traditional approaches to health and well-being as part of a larger resurgence of culture.

The public is also becoming increasingly concerned with the power that pharmaceutical companies have over our ideas about health and healing. Ongoing scandals around the over prescription of drugs like opioids have made many more people open to alternative ways of viewing health. These alternative therapies are also able to offer relief without the side effects which accompany pharmaceutical interventions.

Intractable conditions such as drug addiction, and the ongoing opioid crisis, have illustrated graphically that illness is not simply a physical condition. While there are debilitating physical aspects of addiction, they are clearly the result of larger emotional, environmental, and social economic forces. These conditions also have profound impacts on families and society as a whole putting tremendous pressure on healthcare systems, families and communities.

Trauma research has revealed that for both adults and children experiences of violence, disaster, abuse, and neglect result in a cascade of effects both mental and physical. In children trauma impacts brain and personality development that has an impact on both physical and mental health, and relationships. As a result, effective therapies have been those that sooth and regulate the central nervous system and provide holding environments. This explains why practices that have been used for millenia such as yoga, mindfulness, and drumming, have all proven to be efficacious.

Despite its proven benefits bringing spirituality and religion into conversation with health care has its challenges. Dossey (1993) makes clear that he does not believe physicians should in any way impose their religious beliefs on patients. Describing his own journey from complete rejection of religion he writes:

> But the choice between science and spirituality seems increasingly artificial today, even from a scientific perspective. It is now possible to tell a new story, one that allows science and spirituality to stand side by side in a complimentary way, neither trying to usurp or eliminate the other.
>
> *(p. xx)*

This growing openness allows both healthcare practitioners and those they serve to access the resources of the world's spiritual traditions.

There is an increasingly powerful case being made to include religion and spirituality among other social determinants of health. These include the economic and social conditions necessary to achieve one's aspirations and needs and encompass: political stability, food, shelter, stable ecosystems, education and social support (Raphael, 2016, p. 8). Just as we know that income inequality directly impacts the health of individuals and communities, we now know that religion and spirituality act as a powerful buffer against the many challenges presented by contemporary society.

Increasing openness to a variety of approaches to healing has resulted in the development of various models being suggested. One is the concept of an Integral Approach that emphasizes attention of the four quadrants which include scientifically based research, environmental, economic and social context, and religious and spiritual beliefs and practices.

## REFLECTION

1. Quickly, without overthinking, write down the metaphor or symbol that you would use to represent your body—this can be an animal, an object, a symbol. Jot down whatever comes to mind. Be honest! (If a car, butterfly, or tree comes to mind write it down)
2. What does this metaphor say about your understanding of your body? How does this impact your behaviour in relation to your body?
3. What is your definition of health?

## REFERENCES

Ahmad, Muayyad, Eman Alsman, and Manar Ali-Bani Hani. (2015). Health: A Developing Concept in Nursing. *International Journal of Nursing Studies*. 28 (2), 1–6.

Balboni, Tracy A., Tyler J. Vanderweele, and Stephanie D. Doan-Soares. (2022). Spirituality in Serious Illness and Health. *JAMA*, 328 (2). 184–197.

Coward, Harold and Pinit Ratanakul. (1999). Introduction. In *A Cross-Cultural Dialogue in Health Care Ethics*. Harold Coward and Pinit Ratanakul (Eds.). Wilfrid Laurier University Press.

Crawford, Robert. (1980). Healthism and the Medicalization of Everyday Life. *International Journal of Health Studies*. 10 (3), 365–388.

Dissanayake, Wimal. (1993). Body in Social Theory. In *Self as Body in Asian Theory and Practice*. Thomas P. Kasulis, Roger T. Ames and Wimal Dissanayake (Eds.). State University of New York Press.

Dossey, Larry. (1993). *Healing Words. The Power of Prayer and The Practice of Medicine*. HarperOne.

Durkheim, Émile. (1995). *The Elementary Forms of Religious Life*. Translated with an introduction by Karen E. Fields: Simon and Schuster. Originally published in 1912.

Fields, Gregory P. (2002). *Religious Therapeutics: Body and Health in Yoga, Ayurveda and Tantra*. Motilal Benarsidass.

Freund, P.E.S. and Meredith McGuire. (1999). The Social Construction of Medical Knowledge. In *Health, Illness and the Social Body. A Critical Sociology*. Prentice-Hall.

Griffith, James L. (2012). Psychiatry and Mental Health Treatment. In *Oxford Textbook of Spirituality in Healthcare*. Mark Cobb, Christina M. Puchalski, and Bruce Rumbold (Eds.). Oxford University Press.

Hahn, Robert H. (1995). *Sickness and Healing. An Anthropological Perspective*. Yale University Press.

Levin, Jeff. (2001). *God, Faith and Health. Exploring the Spirituality-Healing Connection*. John Wiley & Sons, Inc.

Ling, Trevor. (1973). *The Buddha. Buddhist Civilization in India and Ceylon*. Maurice Temple Smith Ltd.

Miller, Lisa J. (2016). *The Spiritual Child. The New Science on Parenting for Health and Lifelong Thriving*. St Martin's Press.

Morgan, David. (2010). Introduction. *Religion and Material Culture. The Matter of Belief*. Routledge.

Puchalski, Christina M. and Betty Ferrell. (2010). *Making Health Care Whole. Integrating Spirituality Into Patient Care*. Templeton Press.

Raphael, Dennis. (2016). Social Determinants of Health: Key Issues and Themes. In *Social Determinants of Health. Canadian Perspectives*. Third Edition. Dennis Raphael (Ed.). Canadian Scholars' Press.

Ross, Rupert. (2014). *Indigenous Healing. Exploring Traditional Paths*. Penguin.

*The Encylopedia of Religion*. (1987). Mircea Eliade and Charles J. Adams (Eds). Macmillan.

*The HarperCollins Dictionary of Religion*. (1995). Jonathan Z. Smith (Ed.). HarperCollins.

Thoits, Peggy A. (2011). Mechanisms Linking Social Ties and Support to Physical and Mental Health. *Journal of Health and Social Behavior*. 52 (2), 145–161.

Tillich Paul. (1957). *Dynamics of Faith*. Harper & Bros.

Tsz Ying So, Kyung Young Kim, Emily Kornelsen, Emily Brubaker-Zehr, and Joyce Nyhof-Young. (2023). Teaching Spirituality to Canadian Medical Students: Students' Perceptions of a Spiritual History Taking Clinical Skills Session. *Canadian Medical Education Journal*. 14 (5), 105–107.

Van Der Kolk, Bessel. (2014). *The Body Keeps Score. Brain, Mind, and Body in the Healing of Trauma*. Penguin Books.

Walsh, Froma. (2009). *Spiritual Resources in Family Therapy*. Second Edition. Froma Walsh (Ed). The Guilford Press.

Wehbe-Alamah, Hiba, Linda Sue Hammonds, and David Stanley. (2020). Culturally Congruent Care from the Perspectives of Judaism, Christianity and Islam. *Journal of Transcultural Nursing*. 32 (2), 119–128.

World Health Organization (WHO) Definition of Health, 2023, https://www.publichealth.com.ng/world-health-organizationwho-definition-of-health/

## FURTHER READING

Alexander, Bruce K. (2011). *The Globalization of Addiction. A Study in Poverty of the Spirit*. Oxford University Press. Originally published 2008.

Benson, Herbert and Miriam Z. Klipper. (1975). *The Relaxation Response*. HarperCollins.

Bethune, Brian. (2015). The Science is in. God is the Answer. *Macleans*, April 6 and 15, 2015.

Boyle, Theresa. (2017). Open Pharma Wants Public to Know the Ties Between MDs and Pharmaceutical Industry. *The Toronto Star*, Friday, June 9, 2017.

Davis-Floyd, Robbie F. (1999). Ritual in the Hospital: Giving Birth the American Way. In *Readings in Ritual Studies*. Ronald L. Grimes (Ed.). Prentice-Hall Inc.

Dein, Simon. (2020). Religion, Healing and Mental Health, *Mental Health, Religion and Culture*. 23 (8), 657–665.

Dumit, Joseph. (2012). *Drugs for Life. How Pharmaceutical Companies Define Our Health*. Duke University Press.

Esfahani-Smith, Emily. (2017). *The Power of Meaning. Finding Fulfillment in a World Obsessed with Happiness*. Penguin Canada.

Fontana, David. (2003). *Psychology, Religion and Spirituality*. Blackwell Publishing.

Freund, P.E.S. and Meredith McGuire. (2003). The Social Construction of Medical Knowledge. In *Health, Illness and the Social Body: A Critical Sociology*. 4th Edition. Prentice Hall.

Galanter, M. (2005). *Spirituality and the Healthy Mind: Science Therapy and the Need for Personal Meaning*. Oxford University Press.

Goldberg, Daniel S. (2017). *Public Health Ethics and the Social Determinants of Health*. Cham: Springer Briefs In Public Health.

Griffith. J.L. and Melissa Elliott Griffith. (2002). *Encountering the Sacred in Psychotherapy. How to Talk with People About Their Spiritual Lives*. Guildford Press.

*Handbook of Spirituality, Religion and Mental Health* (2020). David H. Rosmarin and Harold G. Koenig (Eds.). Academic Press.

Herschkopf, Marta, Najmeh Jafari, and Christina Puchalski. (2017). Religions and Spirituality in Medical Education. *Spirituality and Religion Within the Culture of Medicine*. Michael Balboni and John Peteet (Eds.). Oxford University Press.

Johaness, Karl and Ronald Fischer. (2018). Ritual, Repetitiveness and Cognitive Load, A Competitive Test of Ritual Benefits for Stress. *Human Nature*. 29 (4).

Keefe, Patrick Radden. (2021). *Empire of Pain: The Secret History Of the Sackler Dynasty*. Doubleday.

Kinsley, David. (1996). *Health, Healing and Religion. A Cross-Cultural Perspective*. Pearson.

Kleinman, Arthur. (1989). *The Illness Narratives. Suffering, Healing and the Human Condition*. Basic Books.

Koenig, Harold G. (1998). *Handbook of Religion and Mental Health*. Academic Press.

Koithan, Mary. (2019). Concepts and Principles of Integrative Nursing. *Integrative Nursing*. Second Edition. Oxford University Press.

Litalien, Manuel, Dominic Odwa Atari, Ikemdinachi Obasi. (2021). The Influence of Religiosity and Spirituality on Health in Canada: A Systematic Literature Review. *Journal of Religion and Health*. 61 (1), 1–42.

Levin, Jeff. (2009). How Faith Heals: A Theoretical Model. *Explore*. 5 (2), 77–96.

Luchetti, Giancarlo et al. (2021). Spirituality, Religiousness and Mental Health: A Review of the Current Scientific Evidence. *World Journal of Clinical Cases*. 9 (26), 7620–7631.

Marmot, Michael and Richard G. Wilkinson. (2006). *Social Determinants of Health*. Oxford University Press.

Marya, Rupa and Raj Patel. (2021). *Inflamed. Deep Medicine and the Anatomy of Injustice*. Picador, Farrar, Strauss and Giroux.

Mikhail, Alexa. (2023). A Look Inside America's only Blue Zone City—Home to Some of the World's Longest Living People. *Fortune*. April 2, 2023.

Miller, Lisa. (2012/2022). *The Oxford Handbook of Psychology and Spirituality*. Oxford University Press.

Pargament, Kenneth I. (2007). *Spiritually Integrated Psychotherapy*. New The Guildford Press.

Pinker, Susan. (2014). *The Village Effect. How Face-to-Face Contact Can Make Us Healthier and Happier*. Random House.

Puchalski, Christina M. and Betty Ferell. (2010). *Making Health Care Whole. Integrating Spirituality into Patient Care*. Templeton Press.

Raymond, Janice G. (1982). Medicine as Patriarchal Religion. *Journal of Medicine and Philosophy*. 7 (2), 197–216.

Scriber, Susan S., Robert F. Poirier, Wendy Orson, Rose Jackson-Beavers, Booker T. Rice, Karl Wilson, and Barry A. Hong. (2020). Bridges to Care and Recovery. Addressing Behavioral Health Needs Through the Faith Community. *Journal of Religion and Health*. 59 (4), 1946–1957.

Taylor, Elizabeth Johnston. (2019). Health Outcomes of Spiritual and Religious Belief, Behavior and Belonging: Implications for Healthcare Professionals. In *Spirituality in Healthcare. Perspectives for Innovative Practice*. Timmins, F. and Caldeira, S. (Eds). Springer International Publishing.

Taylor, Elizabeth Johnston. (2012). *Religion: A Clinical Guide for Nurses*. Springer.

*The Oxford Handbook to Spirituality and Psychology*. (2012). Lisa J. Miller (Ed.). Oxford University Press.

Young, Caroline and Cyndie Koopsen. (2005). *Spirituality, Health and Healing*. Jones and Bartlett Publishers.

Xygelatas, Dimitris. (2022). *Ritual. How Seemingly Senseless Acts Make Life Worth Living*. Little Brown Spark.

Journal of Religion and Health

Journal of Spirituality in Mental Health

Journal of Transcultural Nursing

Mental Health, Religion & Culture

## INTERNET RESOURCES

Spirituality and Healing, Harvard University Medical School, https://hms.harvard.edu/news/spirituality-healing

TED. (September 2017). “There is More to Life Than Being Happy”/Emily Esfahani-Smith [Video] YouTube, https://www.ted.com/talks/emily_esfahani_smith_there_s_more_to_life_than_being_happy

TED. (2014). “What Makes Us Get Sick? Look Upstream”/ Rishi Manchanda [Video] YouTube, https://www.youtube.com/watch?v=dJEwC4wCM70

The GW Institute for Spirituality and Health: https://smhs.gwu.edu/spirituality-health/

# 2 Tracing the Religious Roots of Biomedicine Through Ancient Egypt and Greece

When an ambulance whizzes by, or walking past a pharmacy, the symbol of the snake wrapped around the caduceus is instantly recognizable. Some of us will have a vague sense of the Greek origins of this symbol. Those working in the fields of medicine or psychology will know that much of the vocabulary is Latin and Greek but not be completely sure of the connection of this image with medicine. The paradoxical relationship that biomedicine maintains with antiquity and with religion can be seen in the ubiquitous symbols we see around us every day.

Tracing the history of western biomedicine leads into a charged and contested area of research. These controversies are linked to the fact that increasingly since the 19th century biomedicine has been at great pains to sever itself from a religious worldview. As Mike Saks (2003) puts it, "modern medicine largely defines itself as non-religious, even anti-religious" (p.151).

Chapters with titles like "Out of Darkness" as seen in monographs such as *A Brief History* of *Medicine: From Hippocrates to Gene Therapy* (2005) are typical of the genre. These works often focus on a depiction of the male heroes of medicine across time from a completely secular standpoint.

The Enlightenment paradigm that frames these narratives constructs the past as a time of darkness out of which science marches

DOI: 10.4324/9781003471769-2

sweeping away the cobwebs of superstition. As a result, in many cases doctors have been trained to bracket out religion and to view it at best as an impediment and at worst as something contemptible. This attitude makes it very challenging to see what can be learned from the past and from traditional practices.

This telling of the story also obscures the relatively new monopoly of biomedicine over health care. The division between medicine and religion was never as clear cut as many works on the history medicine would have us believe. There is no tidy, linear way in which to tell the story of the emergence of what is now understood as biomedicine. Medicine and medical institutions developed differently in various parts of the world with varying degrees of oversight by political and royal powers of the state.

Medical disciplines and sub-disciplines only became iron clad in the 20th century. Tensions between medical doctors and those who practiced other forms of healing increased markedly in the 19th and 20th century as medical doctors claimed more and more authority in the area of health and well-being.

Struggles over who is given the legal right to practice has been a feature of the 20th and 21st centuries. An example from the United States as seen in the Flexner report is instructive in this regard. In 1910 the report calling for the restructuring of medical education resulted in the shutting down of many medical institutions open to African-Americans and women and essentially gave biomedicine a state monopoly over health care.

Policing the boundaries of what is accepted as medicine remains a flashpoint when looking at conflicts over regulation of practices such as Traditional Chinese Medicine or osteopathy and chiropractors. Most of what is now called alternative or complimentary medicine was often referred to as quackery forty years ago.

Despite its clear discomfort with religion, the narrative of the biomedical establishment has generally told the story of western medicine as emerging from the civilization of classical Greece. However, this history posits the Greeks as part of liberation from religion, myth and superstition. Strathern (2005) writes, "it was not until the birth of the scientific outlook in Ancient Greece during the sixth century BC that medicine first took on a rational aspect" (p. 3).

While seeking to retain a connection to ancient Greece the tradition has been carefully cherry picked. And in very telling language the author laments that, "Even so, the ghost of that earlier spirituality continues to haunt medicine" (ibid). This framing of medical history obscures the sophisticated medical systems of the both the ancient world and the fully developed systems of other cultures. As Nutton writes in *Ancient Medicine* (2013), "the legacy of antiquity is still with us" (p. 324).

## HEALING IN ASSYRIA, MESOPOTAMIA, AND ANCIENT EGYPT

A concern with health and the struggle against disease is as old as humanity itself. Remains that have been found of the earliest human beings indicate that they were subject to a variety of illnesses. The development of agriculture resulted in closer proximity to animals and in the transmission of zoonotic diseases to humans.

Growing linkages between groups of people through trade and war also brought human populations increasingly into contact with one another allowing for the spread of contagious diseases. The resulting epidemics in the ancient world profoundly shaped ideas of health and how it could best be achieved and led to the earliest practices of public health strategies.

It is likely the priestly class and shamans acted as the first healers. There is evidence that priest/healers were setting fractures and suturing wounds as early as 40,000 to 30,000 BCE. In civilizations such as Mesopotamia and Egypt, starting in the 4th century BCE, medical schools were attached to temples and the salaries of doctors were paid by the ruler. The physicians of Mesopotamia and Assyria were often connected with temples complexes and their records reveal an awareness of hygiene, diagnostic measures, and contagious disease.

Medical records indicate that Egyptian doctors were performing surgeries from 3000 BCE onward. These works were associated with the Egyptian God Thoth, who came to be known as Hermes in Greek. Unfortunately, the Book of Thoth has never been discovered in its entirety and it is thought that one of the last copies was destroyed in the destruction of the Library at Alexandria in the 4th century CE.

The *Book of Thoth* consisted of 42 papyrus scrolls which were believed to have been dictated by the God himself. These writings covered a wide range of topics including: astrology, astronomy, hymns to Thoth, and treatises on philosophy and medicine as well as descriptions of ceremonial practices. Imhotep the chief physician to the pharaoh Djoser was deified and later identified with the Greek God of Healing, Asclepius.

Doctors in ancient Egypt were part of an elite class who had access to these sacred and esoteric texts. These early forms of medicine emerged from and were contained within a religious worldview and notions of cleanliness and sanitation were developed from a desire for ritual purity. Medical services in ancient Egypt were often provided free of charge by the state.

By the 3rd century BCE religiously based and empirical-rationalist medicine existed side by side in Egypt. Evidence indicates that there was a group of physicians, some of whom the records indicate were women, who were performing surgery. Each specialization had a patron god or goddess and it was understood that the physician worked under the auspices of the deity.

Large temples at Dendera, Deir el-Bahri and Philaee in Egypt during the Graeco-Roman period in the 4th century CE were used for both religious and therapeutic purposes. At Denderas a sacred lake and sanatorium welcomed visitors who were anointed with water that had been poured over healing statues. There was also a room dedicated to the deified physician Imhotep. The Egyptian temple-maintained gardens for the growing of medicinal herbs and kept large collections of medical writings.

When the Persians invaded Egypt in the 5th century BCE Darius commanded the Chief Physician of Egypt to arrest the decline in medical practice:

> His Majesty King Darius commanded me to return to Egypt in order to restore the department of the House (s) of Life after (they had fallen) into decay… I equipped them with all their ability and all their apparatus which was needed in accordance with their former condition. His Majesty did this because he knew the value of the art to revive all that are sick and to commemorate forever the name (s) of all the gods.
>
> *(Gardiner, 1938, pp. 157–8)*

The available medical papyri indicate the ancient Egyptians practiced a wide variety of techniques and left written records discussing: surgery, the structure of the body, diseases, instruments of doctors, remedies, diseases of the eyes, diseases of women (Nunn, 1996, p. 24). The Kahn papyri focus on gynecological issues and nurses and midwives were also trained within these systems.

## MEDICINE IN ANCIENT GREECE

Close connections existed between ancient Greek medicine and Egypt as Greek imperialism spread its culture as far as North Africa. In ancient Greece physicians often travelled from town to town building up a clientele by first treating the poor of the community for free and were often paid by taxation. Physicians were valuable to the Greeks state as they healed the soldiers who fought in the wars of empire. As a result, some Greek city states hired physicians as civil servants.

The Greek god most associated with healing is Asclepius. According to myth, he was the son of Apollo the God of healing and was trained by the wise centaur, Chiron. Over time, he became known as the god of medicine with his own cult and temples. Hartigan (2009) makes the point that Asclepius, who is generally depicted as a middle-aged man wearing a cloak and carrying a staff, "shows consistent kindness" to mortals. In this way he is unlike the other Greek gods who are as likely to send suffering as to cure it (p. 21). Asclepius remains an archetype of the "good doctor" who is compassionate and committed to the welfare of the patient.

In the mythology Asclepius is aided by his daughters Hygeia and Panacae from which our words hygiene and panacea are derived. This demonstrates both the sacred nature of purity and the recognition of the link between cleanliness and health. It also illustrates the idea that well-being requires a constellation of aspects including lifestyle, diet and herbs to create optimum health.

As in ancient Egypt healing centres grew up within the Greek world and were referred to as Asclepeia. They functioned as centres of medical advice, prognosis, and healing. These healing sanctuaries were dedicated to the god of medicine, were established throughout Greece, usually in settings of awe-inspiring natural beauty and scenic grandeur. The main Asclepion was in Epidaurus, with important branches in Cos and Pergamum (see Appendix 2).

Schools were attached to the temples of Asclepius and most physicians lived in a specific quarter of the town. The snake was associated with the God Asclepius and the Greek sign for an Asclepiad was a staff entwined with a snake. The members of this guild were typically trained as apprentices often by their own fathers and upon completion of their training had to swear the Hippocratic oath.

## HIPPOCRATES AND GALEN AS MODEL DOCTORS

The figure who looms largest in the ancient Greek medical world is Hippocrates (*c*.460–375 BCE), often regarded as the model of the ideal physician and "father of medicine". He was born on the island of Cos, Greece and according to traditional narrative his father was a physician/ priest at the Asclepion at Cos. Hippocrates is understood as embodying the qualities of compassion, intelligence, ethical integrity, and honesty expected of a doctor.

Hippocrates left behind approximately 60 texts referred to as the *Corpus Hippocraticum*. This Hippocratic Corpus has had an unprecedented influence and represented the touchstone for medical training in the western up to the modern period. The corpus continues to inspire healers in the present as it emphasizes the role of clean water, fresh air, daily exercise, and proper diet in maintaining good health. For this reason, Hippocrates is claimed both by allopathic doctors and alternative healers as an antecedent and role model.

The works of Hippocrates include a pharmocopeaia, descriptions of surgery and observation of symptoms and diagnosis with case studies included. These elements existed alongside religious rituals and practices and as Nutton (2013) notes, "religion and secular healing reinforced rather than opposed each other" (p. 115). Discussing the need for prognosis, Hippocrates wrote:

> I hold that it is an excellent thing for a physician to practice forecasting. For if he discover and declare unaided by the side of his patients the present, the past and the future, and fill in the gap given by the sick, he will be the more believed to understand cases, so that men will confidently entrust themselves to him for treatment. Furthermore, he will carry out the treatment best if he know beforehand from present symptoms what will take place later.
>
> *(Fergren and Lomperis, 2017, pp. 53–4)*

Hippocrates' recognition of the need to inform the patient of their condition and likely outcomes remains a central feature of contemporary medicine.

Galen (129–216 CE) is the other figure in ancient Greece who is typically viewed by western medicine as a founder of the biomedical tradition. Galen also bridges the ancient Greek into the Roman world. The son of a wealthy architect, Galen was born in the Greek city of Pergamum (now Turkey) also the site of an Asclepion and where he studied medicine.

Galen studied medicine in Pergamum and in Alexandria. which was considered to be the greatest medical centre of the ancient world. Upon moving to Rome Galen rapidly developed a reputation as a gifted practitioner and ultimately became court physician to the Roman emperor Marcus Aurelius (*c.*160–180 CE).

Galen regarded anatomy as the foundation of medical knowledge, although taboos against dissecting human bodies resulted in inaccuracies in his mapping of the body. Galen's advocacy of dissection, both to improve surgical skills and for research purposes, was extremely influential. He distinguished seven pairs of cranial nerves, described the valves of the heart, and observed the structural differences between arteries and veins.

Alongside his many discoveries in the field of anatomy, Galen believed in both a divine order and the healing powers of nature. Invoking the names of both Plato and Hippocrates in *The Usefulness of the Parts of the Body* he composed hymns in praise of the Creator emphasizing the role of the wisdom and goodness emerging from the divine order.

Galen's skill and egotism are both noted by the historical record and it includes various boasts regarding his abilities as a healer. However, he has continued to inspire contemporary medicine with his emphasis on the importance of the doctor/patient relationship and need for trust between the two. He also focused on the need to listen carefully to patients and to use reason, observation, and intuition to help in healing.

The outlines of the good doctor are clearly still in place and no doubt why these figures have remained important within western medical training. Doctors as depicted in popular television programmes such as *House* can clearly be seen as embodying many of the same traits as their ancient ancestors with equal parts eccentricity, ego, and compassion.

In his history of western medicine Bynum (2008) outlines the key inheritances that remain from ancient Greek approaches to healing. These include the ideas of moderation and balance in diet and lifestyle, the healing power of nature, and environmental factors in health. They also include a tradition of the caring physician who teaches and mentors others and leaves a written record of research. The medical tradition has also maintained the practice of observation of the symptoms and an empirical approach, and the principle of "if not to help than to do no harm".

## THE HIPPOCRATIC OATH

I swear by Apollo the physician, and Aesculapius, and Health, and All-heal, and all the gods and goddesses, that, according to my ability and judgment, I will keep this Oath and this stipulation—to reckon him who taught me this Art equally dear to me as my parents, to share my substance with him, and relieve his necessities if required; to look upon his offspring in the same footing as my own brothers, and to teach them this Art, if they shall wish to learn it, without fee or stipulation; and that by precept, lecture, and every other mode of instruction, I will impart a knowledge of the Art to my own sons, and those of my teachers, and to disciples bound by a stipulation and oath according to the law of medicine, but to none others. I will follow that system of regimen which, according to my ability and judgment, I consider for the benefit of my patients, and abstain from whatever is deleterious and mischievous. I will give no deadly medicine to any one if asked, nor suggest any such counsel; and in like manner I will not give to a woman a pessary to produce abortion. With purity and with holiness I will pass my life and practice my Art. I will not cut persons laboring under the stone, but will leave this to be done by men who are practitioners of this work. Into whatever houses I enter, I will go into them for the benefit of the sick, and will abstain from every voluntary act of mischief and corruption; and, further from the seduction of females or males, of freemen and slaves. Whatever, in connection with my professional practice or not, in connection with it, I see or hear, in the life of men, which ought not to be spoken of abroad, I will not divulge, as reckoning that all such should be kept secret. While I continue to keep this Oath unviolated, may it be granted to me to enjoy life and the practice of the art, respected by all men, in all times! But should I trespass and violate this Oath, may the reverse be my lot!

## Higher Values vs. the Marketplace: The Continuing Importance of the Hippocratic Oath in Medical Ethics

In 1996 Dr Nancy Olivieri found herself a lightning rod for the larger controversies swirling around corporate funding of drug trials and medical ethics. Dr Olivieri, one of the world's leading researchers in blood diseases, was overseeing clinical trials of a new drug called deferiprone (L1) meant for patients of the blood disorder thalassemia. Upon discovering potential hazards of the drug, she immediately moved to inform participants in the trails. What followed eventually brought Dr. Olivieri to international attention as the sponsoring drug company invoked a secrecy clause and threatened a multimillion-dollar lawsuit.

At the same time a similar controversy was being played out around Dr. Betty Dong a pharmacological researcher at the University of California. Dong's findings regarding a thyroid medication were blocked by legal action taken by the pharmaceutical company sponsoring her research. The company finally relented after seven years and the results were published in 1997.

Both Dong and Olivieri were threatened legally for attempting to protect the public and exposed the tangled web of relationships between research and corporate interests. This entanglement was related to the reduction in government funds for medical research and the increased dependence on drug companies for funding.

In the Olivieri case the Canadian Association of University Teachers (CAUT) moved in to support her and submitted a report stating that she had fulfilled her ethical obligations. The report also made 31 recommendations including:

- Contracts involving industrial sponsorship of clinical research should never prevent researchers from informing patients or the scientific community of any risks.
- All universities and affiliated teaching hospitals should have in place policies and practices that are effective in protecting academic freedom, as well as principles of research and clinical ethics.
- Health Canada should review the current regulation of health research and make appropriate changes to protect the public interest and the rights of patients who volunteer to be subjects of research.

In 2001 The Canadian College of Physician and Surgeons of Ontario exonerated Dr. Olivieri stating, "The Committee concurs with the panel in finding that use of the drug was terminated in a timely and expedient fashion, in the best interests of Dr. Olivieri's patients" (CSPO 2001, p. 19).

In the years since the case was resolved larger ethical issues around research and the often close ties between pharmaceutical companies and research have come under increased scrutiny. All researchers who publish are now required to publicly acknowledge any ties to corporate sponsorship.

These cases, which threatened both the careers and reputations of these courageous researchers were pivotal in bringing about these changes. Traditional medical codes have had to come into dialogue with newer codes springing from the discourses of Human Rights after World War Two such as the Nuremberg Code.

As Schafer (2004) concludes, "Even if Nancy Olivieri were *legally* bound to keep confidential all information about the risks of deferiprone, she was *morally* obliged to disclose that information to her patients and to her colleagues worldwide. It could be argued, of course, that one has a moral obligation to keep the contracts one signs. This moral obligation is prima facie, however, rather than absolute, and should surely be overridden where the lives and health of patients are at stake" (p. 11).

Increasingly medical schools have strict conflict of interest guidelines for doctors and researchers. Having a sense of the higher order values embodied in the Hippocratic Oath and Nuremberg Code of Medical Ethics ensures that those working in the medical field understand where their first loyalty lies. The emphasis on "doing no harm" continues to inspire and guide medical doctors in navigating challenging situations such as these. Drs Olivieri and Dong became internationally admired for upholding the highest ethics of their professions.

## REFERENCES

Bynum, William. (2008). *The History of Medicine: A Very Short Introduction*. Oxford University Press.

Fergren, Gary B. and Ekaterina N. Lomperis. (2017). *Essential Readings in Medicine and Religion*. The John Hopkins University Press.

Gardiner, Alan H. (1938, December). The House of Life. *The Journal of Egyptian Archaeology*. 24 (2), 83–91.

Hartigan, Karelisa V. (2009). *Performance and Cure. Drama and Healing In Ancient Greece and Contemporary America*. Duckworth.

Nunn, John F. (1996). *Ancient Egyptian Medicine*. University of Oklahoma Press.

Nutton, Vivian. (2013). *Ancient Medicine*. Second Edition. Routledge.

Saks, Mike. (2003). *Orthodox and Alternative Medicine: Politics, Professionalization and Health Care*. Contiuum.

Schafer A. (2004). Biomedical Conflicts of Interest: A Defense of Sequestration Thesis-learning from the Case of Nancy Olivieri and David Healy. *Journal of Medical Ethics*. 30 (8), 8–24.

Strathern, Paul. (2005). *A Brief History of Medicine from Hippocrates to Gene Therapy*. Robinson.

*The Olivieri Report*. (2001). A CAUT Series. James Lorimer and Company.

## FURTHER READING

Belluz, Julia. (2013). Students Demand Boundaries between Drug Firms and Medical Schools: The Push to Go Pharma-free after a Series of Scandals, *Macleans*, September 23, 2013.

Bynum, William. (2006). *The Western Medical Tradition. 1800–2000*. Cambridge University Press.

*CSPO Complaints Committee Decision*, December 19, 2001.

*Diagnosis in Assyrian and Babylonian Medicine. Ancient Sources, Translations and Analyses*. (2005). JoAnn Scurlock (Trans) and Burton R. Andersen. University of Chicago Press.

Elotoria, Ibrahim M. (2020). *A Spotlight on the History of Ancient Egyptian Medicine*. CRC Press, Taylor & Francis.

Fergren, Gary B. (2014). *Medicine and Religion. A Historical Introduction*. The John Hopkins University Press.

Forest, M. and G. Hart. (2000). *Asclepius the God of Medicine*. Royal Society of Medicine Press.

Ghalioungui, Paul. (1963). *Magic and Medical Science in Ancient Egypt*. London: Hodder and Staughton.

Jackson, Stanley W. (Spring, 2001). The Wounded Healer. *Bulletin of the History of Medicine*, 75 (1), 1–36.

Jackson, Stanley W. (1981). American and Canadian Medical Institutions.1800–1870. *Medicine in Canadian Society. Historical Perspectives*. S.E.D. Short (Ed.). McGill Queen's University Press.

*Magic and Rationality in Ancient and Near Eastern and Graeco-Roman Medicine*. (2004). Manfred Horstmanshoff and Marten Stol (Eds.) Brill.

Mauceri, Joseph. (1986). *The Great Break: A Short History of the Separation of Medical Sciences and Religion*. Pulse.

Maugh, Thomas H. (1997). Drug Firm Suppressed Test Data for Years, Doctors Say. *Los Angeles Times*, April 16, 1997.

Nancy Olivieri Speaks to Lesley Stahl, *The Secrecy Clause*, 60 Minutes, December 19, 1999.

Olivieri Medical Dispute Settled, *The Canadian Encyclopedia*. https://www.thecanadianencyclopedia.ca/en/article/olivieri-medical-dispute-settled

Reeves, Carole. (1992). *Egyptian Medicine*. Shire.

Savitt, Todd. (September, 2006). Abraham Flexner and the Black Medical Schools. *Journal of the National Medical Association*, 98 (9), 1415–24.

Saunders, J. B. de C. (1963). *The Transitions from Ancient Egyptian to Greek Medicine*. Logan Clendening Lectures on the History and Philosophy of Medicine. University of Kansas Press.

Smith, Virginia. (2007). *Clean. A History of Personal Hygiene and Purity*. Oxford University Press.

Strouhal, Eugen, Bretislav Vachala, and Hana Vymazalová. (2021). *Medicine of the Ancient Egyptians: 2. Internal Medicine*. American University in Cairo Press.

*The Nuremberg Code. Directives for Human Experimentation*: https://muhc.ca/sites/default/files/users/user136/The%20Nuremberg%20Code.pdf

*The Routledge Handbook of Religion, Medicine and Health*. (2022). Dorothea Luddeckens (Ed.). Routledge.

Watson, Claire. (2022). Undisclosed Industry Payments Rampant in Drug-trial Papers. A Quarter of Medical Researchers Involved in Clinical Trials in Australia did not Declare Funding from Pharmaceutical Companies. *Nature*, March 24, 2022.

*Western Medical Thought from Antiquity to the Middle Ages*. (2002). Mirko D. Gromedke (Ed.). Translated by Antony Shugari. Harvard University Press.

Yoshikama, Naoi Kukita. (2015). *Medicine, Religion and Gender in Medical Culture*. Boydell & Brenner Ltd.

# 3 Technologies of the Sacred: Shamanism and Neo-Shamanism in the Contemporary World

The practices of shamanism include some of the oldest forms of healing recorded in human history. The shaman was probably the first, outside of the family circle, to take on a specialist function as healer. He or she served as a counselor, storyteller, poet, diviner, clairvoyant among many other roles. While the word shaman is derived from Siberian languages, this figure can be found in various forms across the world cultures.

The practices and worldview developed within shamanism continue to be used in almost all healing settings, knowingly or unknowingly, and have much to tell us about holistic forms of healing. Despite direct attacks under Communist regimes in the Soviet Union and attempts at conversion in other parts of the world, shamans continue to practice in Indigenous cultures around the globe, and in traditions spanning across Africa to Asia.

The development of forms of neo-shamanism also speak to a growing understanding that the worldview and techniques of these healers can be used to address contemporary issues. The bringing

DOI: 10.4324/9781003471769-3

together of psychology, psychosomatic healing, relationship with nature and the role of community within the shamanic approach offers a vital corrective to the fragmented and alienated vision of so much of our healthcare system.

Anthropologist Fiona Bowie (2006) notes that, 'most writers agree that "shamanism is a technique rather than a religion" (p. 191). However, the outlines of the "shamanic complex" have a great deal to offer in terms of illustrating key elements of healing that recur again and again across human culture. Because of this it remains a useful if contested term. The recurrence of concepts such as the wounded healer and the idea of healing as a vocation across time and culture speak to the deep structures of the human psyche.

Shamanistic practices offer a holistic perspective that includes relationship to community, non- human persons, and the world of nature. This ancient paradigm also brings us back into dialogue with expanded states of consciousness and body work. It makes sense, then, to start with the powerful and fascinating figure of the shaman.

## THE SHAMAN AS ARCHETYPAL HEALER

The shaman has been described as being a, "physician, magician, counselor and protector" (Bouse, 2019, p. 4). In his pioneering work *Shamanism: the Archaic Techniques of Ecstasy* (2020) Mircea Eliade was one of the first academics to study these practices. This work spans over two and a half millennia of human history, moving from the shamanic traditions of Siberia and Central Asia to North and South America, Indonesia, Africa, Tibet, China, and beyond.

Building on this research anthropologist Michael Harney developed the idea of "core shamanism" which looks at features of these practices that can be found across culture. Harney bridges the study of traditional forms of shamanism and neo-shamanism in creating the Foundation for Shamanic Studies in 1979 in California. Since then, numerous centres and foundations dedicated to teaching forms of neo-shamanism have sprung up across North America.

Shamanism is based fundamentally on the idea that certain people have a particular gift for gaining access to the spirit realm. This ability often comes about as the result of a near death experience. A life-threatening sickness in this context is understood as an initiation and the spirits way of calling the person to their vocation.

The biographies of shamans tend to look remarkably similar—generally in that the person is afflicted with a serious illness either mental/physical breakdown or both in late adolescence. This may result in a near-death experience during which their family and community believe that they have died.

There is often a motif of the dismemberment and complete reconfiguration of the body leading to rebirth as a shaman. Eliade (2020) says of these stories, "Taken together, they represent a well-organized variant of the universal theme of the death and mystical resurrection of the candidate by means of a descent to the underworld and an ascent to the sky" (p. 43).

This experience of having died and returned to life is a central motif in the life of the shaman. Because of this return from the land of the spirits he or she understands the "geography of death", and can act as a mediator between the spiritual and mundane world. Just as importantly he or she is not afraid of the realm of death and can aid others in negotiating soul loss and illness. Having returned from the dead, the shaman is also believed to possess the gifts of healing.

Once selected, the initiate learns how to fulfill their role through dreams, trances and visions and through instruction in the mythology and study of history. Through this process the pre-choice individual is transformed into "a technician of the sacred" (Eliade, 2020). The shaman may also act as an apprentice to a senior shaman, but the emphasis is on the power/charisma derived from one's own ordeal and inward experience.

There is a vast body of techniques used that can include drumming, singing, storytelling, counseling, and dream interpretation. Practices may also include the use of hallucinogenic drugs always consumed in a ritualized setting. Once in a trance state they can determine the cause of a person's illness.

Once trained, shamans possess a wide repertoire of rituals to facilitate healing and include: divination, dream interpretation, dancing often while wearing masks and costumes so for instance dramatizing the descent into the realm of the spirits. They may also use a variety of extremely practical skills such as knowledge of medicinal plants, bone-setting, and massage.

From this perspective there is a sense of kinship with all aspects of the natural world. There is also a profound sense of the importance of place and the unity of the community of all living beings in that particular place. In many cases the shaman has an animal guide who leads them through visionary landscapes, to the World Tree that connects the three realms of Heaven, Earth, and Underworld.

## *Tale of the Shaman*

Sick with smallpox, the future shaman remained unconscious for three days and so nearly dead that on the third day he was almost buried. His initiation took place during this time. He remembered having been carried into the middle of a sea. There he heard his Sickness (that is, smallpox) speak saying to him, "From the Lords of the Water you will receive the gift of shamanizing. Your name as a shaman will be Huottarie (Diver)". …

When they came to high place, the guides showed him seven tents with torn roofs. He entered the first and there found the inhabitants of the underworld and the men of the Great Sickness (syphilis). These men tore out his heart and threw it into a pot. In other tents he met the Lord of Madness and the Lords of all the nervous disorders, as well as the evil shamans. Thus, he learned the various diseases that torment mankind …

Still preceded by his guides, the candidate then came to the Land of the Shamanesses, who strengthened his throat and his voice. He was then carried to the shores of the Nine Seas. In the middle of one of them was an island, and in the middle of the island a young birch tree rose to the sky. It was the Tree of the Lord of the Earth. Beside it grew nine herbs, the ancestors of all the plants on earth.

(Eliade, 2020, p. 39)

The regalia of the shaman plays an important role as the clothing reflects an intimate relationship with the natural and spirit worlds which are interpenetrating. The clothing of the shaman represents a whole worldview and "discloses not only a sacred presence but also cosmic symbols" (Eliade, 2020, p. 90). Like all uniforms these forms of clothing demarcate a particular role and status in society.

This apparel, which also serves a protective function, is of completely different order to contemporary views of clothing which are mass produced. While the vital role of clothing often goes unremarked in our society, scholarly works such as Richard Thompson Ford's *Dress Codes* (2021) demonstrates the symbolic, social and political power of modes of dress. The well-known authority of the white coat of the doctor speaks to the continued power of apparel.

As David Kinsley (1996) argues, the roles of contemporary healers such as physicians, nurses, counselors and psychologists often contain shamanic elements whether the practitioner is aware of it or not. The importance of the relationship between the patient and healer remains at the centre of medical practice and is dependent on good communication and mutual respect and trust (Kinsley, 1996, p. 153).

This approach to healing recognizes that what healers do often involves responsibilities and levels of commitment that move them outside the parameters of a solely mundane economic activity. The figure of the shaman embodies the understanding of the role of the healer as a vocation. When moving within the realm of mortality, suffering, illness, and pain, many practitioners recognize that working in the field of healing is more than just a career.

This is generally recognized in the caring professions, whether or not the understanding is explicitly religious. Observing the selfless actions of nurses, doctors, and other healthcare workers in times of war, famine, and pandemic clearly illustrates there is a motivation beyond profit or status for many practitioners. Working with people in these deepest dimensions of human experience can be transformative for the physician, "it may cause us to see health care as a spiritual path and ourselves as spiritual beings" (Remen, 2010, p. xvii).

The role of the Wounded Healer also appears again and again among those who work as healers. Those who have undergone their own experiences of illness, addiction, pain, and recovery are often especially effective. The idea of the wounded healer is someone who has transmuted their own suffering in to "a sensitivity to the suffering of others" (Jackson, 2001, p.36).

In *Making Health Care Whole* (2010) Remen writes that healthcare professionals, "often meet people at the thresholds of the world, welcoming them when they are born and letting go of their hands as they die". And while their vocation leads them into these places of existential meaning, "Little in our training prepares us to have comfort with the unknown or even to recognize the spiritual nature of such meetings" (xv).

## REFLECTION

1. What qualities do you think are necessary to be an effective healer?

2. Why do you think the dyad of patient and healer remains so important?
3. How does a vocation or calling differ from a career or job? How is this relevant to a career in healing?
4. Why do you think the wounded healer remains such a powerful idea?

## NEO-SHAMANISM: ANCIENT WISDOM AND CONTEMPORARY CHALLENGES

Alongside the continued practice of shamanism in its traditional forms "neo-shamanism" has grown in popularity since the 1980s. This movement uses shamanic techniques such as drumming, storytelling, altered states of consciousness, and soul journeying. These practices are often used as an adjunct to therapy, counseling, and social work. These approaches have proven to be very effective in particularly in work with trauma and addiction.

As Van der Kolk (2014) has argued, no amount of intellectual insight will help when a person is a state of heightened arousal and post-traumatic stress syndrome (PTSD). He notes that social support is vital to protecting against stress and trauma but, "many traumatized people find themselves chronically out of synch with the people around them" (p. 81). Shared activities that don't require conversation are particularly effective in working with those who have suffered trauma.

Neo-shamanism has proven successful with syndromes that clearly have physical, mental, and emotional components such as addiction and so cannot be just treated simply as a physical ailment. We may know in detail the biological impacts of substance abuse while remaining powerless to cope with how to heal people of addiction. Addictions also illustrate the ways in which the illness of one person impacts their large social circles as they have serious impacts on whole family systems and on communities.

Shamanic techniques have proven to be effective with those who do not respond well to talk therapy such as young men who are generally trained by their society not to express vulnerability or emotion. Neo-shamanic practices can include percussion and singing and storytelling rather than focusing on verbal self-disclosure.

Neo-shamanism acknowledges the existence and importance of altered states of consciousness in healing and these techniques have proven effective in offering alternatives to drug use. These mental states, akin to those produced by meditation, offer a form of relaxation and respite from challenging mental states or flashbacks. With this approach this is achieved without the need to sit still for long periods of time—something challenging for most people but especially for adolescents.

Drumming and dancing emphasize self-expression and can contribute to rebuilding emotional health in a way that is non-threatening and enjoyable. Use of sound and motion allows for an embodied practice and soothes the sympathetic nervous system. Learning to self-soothe in a healthy way is a vital part of treating addiction.

Practices derived from shamanism recognize that past experiences are held in the body as well as in the mind. Techniques grounded in the body mitigate feelings of dissociation and depersonalization that are common results of trauma. Neo-shamanic practices help ground the person in their body and help develop synchrony, emotional regulation, and social cooperation.

Because many who struggle with addiction are often disconnected and feel isolated even around other people practices such drumming helps create a sense of connectedness. Addictions counselor Seaman says. "All of us need this reconnection to ourselves, to our soul, to a higher power. Drums bring this out. Drums penetrate people at a deeper level. Drumming produces a sense of connectedness and community, integrating body, mind and spirit." (Winkelman, 2003, p. 648).

Programmes using neo-shamanic practices have been offered in colleges, after-school programmes, group homes, and at psychology and addiction conferences. Shamanic practices can also be a useful addition to pre-existing programmes such as Alcoholic Anonymous (AA) and can be used counsellors and social workers in a wide variety of settings including: private practice, prisons, mental health centres, schools, and community centres.

The world view and practices of shamanism continue to be vital and effective, whether in traditional or re-imagined forms. The shamanic complex contains within it some of the most vital aspects of healing including emphasizing the close relationship between healer and patient, use of various states of consciousness, the holistic understanding of human health that takes in all the many of dimensions of human life including community, the spirit the natural world.

## *Myron Eshowsky: Spiritual Healer and Shaman*

Myron Eshowsky was trained both in psychology and as a shamanic counselor at the Foundation for Shamanic Studies in Novato, California. Beginning in the mid-1980s he has worked in a range of settings from inpatient psychiatric facilities, acute care settings to private practice, community mental health centres, and prisons.

Eshowsky's successes led the drug/alcohol unit of his agency to refer clients with a history of severe addiction and significant mental health issues to him. He subsequently worked with at-risk youth and gangs at an and provided programmes for mental health centres, community-based antiviolence groups, and hospitals.

## *Example of a Shaman's journey: Journey to the Lower World*

(This practice is done with the accompaniment of drumming either live or recorded. You are encouraged to keep a journal of your experiences. Find a dark and quiet space where you can relax and become receptive.)

Close your eyes and begin to focus on an opening in the earth that you will want to enter in your imagination. … Spend time connecting with this place in your mind. … In this journey you will be seeking to go to a world beneath the surface of the earth to meet a helping animal spirit. …

Remember that any time our mind wanders or you get caught up in internal dialogue about whether you are doing it right, repeat your intention— "I am going to the lower world to meet a helping animal spirit and ask for help in feeling stronger and more alive". …

Enter your entrance point into the earth and begin to go down a tunnel. … You are entering a state where time is stopped and all is possible. Once you see a light at the end of the tunnel and exit, begin to look for a helping animal spirit. Any animal you see, simply ask, "Are you my helping animal spirit?" In some way, directly or indirectly, you will get an answer. If it's "no" then move on until you meet the animal that is working with you.

When you meet the animal helper, let it know you are there to ask for help in feeling stronger and alive. From that point on anything that happens in the journey will be your spiritual answer to the question, so pay careful attention to the setting and to everything that occurs.

At some point, the drumming will change to signal an end to the journey. When that happens, return in a conscious way the same way you entered the lower world. Before leaving, thank the helping spirit(s) for the help you received. If it feels right, ask what you can do in return to help the spirits. Right relationship requires a sense of honor and respect, and is reciprocal in nature. Remember to return up the tunnel to the entry point where you started. Once back in this realm, take time to reflect on your experiences.

—from *Flourishing World In Action: Dreaming the World Anew*, Myron Eshowsky, unpublished with permission of the author.

## REFLECTIONS

1. Why do you think neo-shamanism has become an increasingly popular approach to healing?
2. Does music and art have a role to play in healing?
3. Why do you think neo-shamanism is so effective in working with adolescents?

## REFERENCES

Bouse, Karel James. (2019). *Neo-shamanism and Mental Health*. Palgrave Macmillan.

Bowie, Fiona. (2006). Shamanism. *The Anthropology of Religion. An Introduction*. Blackwell Publishers Inc.

Eliade, Mircea. (2020). *Shamanism: Archaic Techniques of Ecstasy*. Princeton University Press. Originally published in 1951.

Ford, Richard Thompson. (2021). *Dress Codes: How the Laws of Fashion Made History*. Simon & Schuster Paperbacks.

Jackson, Stanley W. (Spring, 2001). The Wounded Healer. *Bulletin of the History of Medicine*, 75 (1), 1–36.

Kinsley, David. (1996). *Health, Healing and Religion. A Cross-Cultural Perspective*. Prentice Hall.

Remen, Naomi. (2010). Foreword. *Making Health Care Whole*. Templeton Press.

Van Der Kolk, Bessell. (2014). *The Body Keeps The Score: Brain, Mind and Body In the Healing of Trauma*. Penguin Books.

Winkelman, Michael. (April 2003). Complementary Therapy for Addiction: Drumming Out the Drugs. *American Journal of Public Health*, 93 (4), 647–51.

## FURTHER READING

Actherberg, Jeanne. (1985). *Imagery in Healing: Shamansim and Modern Medicine*. Shambhala.

Boon-ooi Lee, Laurence Kimayer and Danielle Groleau. (March 2010). "Therapeutic Processes and Perceived Helpfulness of Dag Ki (Chinese Shamanism) from the Symbolic Healing Perspective." *Culture, Medicine and Psychiatry*. 34 (1), 56–105.

DuBois, Thomas A. (2009). *An Introduction to Shamanism*. Cambridge University Press.

Eliade, Mircea. (2020). *Shamanism: Archaic Techniques of Ecstasy*, Princeton University Press. Originally published in 1951.

Harner, Michael. (1980). *The Way of the Shaman*. HarperSanFrancisco.

Ingerman, Sandra. (1991). *Soul Retrieval. Mending the Fragmented Self*. Harper Collins.

Kim, Chongho. (2018). *Korean Shamanism: The Cultural Paradox*. Routledge. Originally published in 2003.

Oosten, J. G. and Laugrand, Frédéric. (2010). *Inuit Shamanism and Christianity: Transitions and Transformations in the Twentieth Century*. McGill-Queen's University Press.

Sarfati, Liora. (2021). *Korean Shamanism. From Ritual to Digital*. Indiana University Press.

Singh, Manvir. (2018). The Cultural Evolution of Shamanism. *Behavioral and Brain Sciences*, 41, e99.

Thomas, Michael. (September 2017). Shamanism Theory and the Early Chinese "Wu". *Journal of the American Academy of Religion*, 83 (3), 649–96.

Watson-Jones, Rachel E., and Christine H. Legare. (2018). The Social Functions of Shamanism. *The Behavioural and Brain Sciences*. 41.

Wallis, Robert J. (2012). Journeying the Politics of Ecstasy: Anthropological Perspectives on Neoshamanism. *Pomegranite*. 13 (6), 20–28.

# 4 Maintaining the Spiritual Centre: Indigenous Approaches to Health and Healing

The word Indigenous is an umbrella term used to describe unique cultures and ways of relating to community and the environment. Indigenous nations and communities across the globe have retained social, cultural, economic, and political characteristics that are distinct from those of the dominant societies in which they live. Often this includes cultural forms, legal and ceremonial systems that are held orally, a sense of sacred relationship to place and reverence for the natural world.

The term Indigenous emerged from political movements across the world that made common cause as groups most impacted by colonization and modern practices of mining, logging, and resource extraction. While the Maori of New Zealand, the Aborigines of Australia, and many First Nations people of both North and South America are all distinct traditions they recognize a common experience of attempted assimilation and genocide. This has included the seizing of land, destruction of food sources and languages, and spiritual and religious traditions.

No discussion of Indigenous approaches to health and wellbeing can ignore the context of colonialism which had an immediate and catastrophic impact beginning with first contact in the 15th century. For the past 500 years many of the world's Indigenous traditions have existed in close contact with world religions such as

DOI: 10.4324/9781003471769-4

Christianity, Islam, and Buddhism. In many cases this has resulted in syncretic approaches to religion and spirituality.

The decades following the 1960s saw rise of movements that called for a reclaiming and return to original spiritual and cultural practices. The resurgence of traditional practices in Indigenous communities across North America points to the potent power of spirituality to heal and uphold communities.

The United Nations Declaration on the Rights of Indigenous Peoples has recognized the separate status of Indigenous cultures. As a group Indigenous groups have worked with the UN and have lobbied the Vatican for the withdrawal of the Doctrine of Discovery and the rejection of the idea of Terra Nullius which stated that any land that was not inhabited by Christians was open to settlement. These two concepts were the charters of colonial conquest throughout the world and were officially withdrawn by the Vatican in 2023.

The connection between health and well-being and political and social systems, and economics is shown with stark clarity in the case of the health of Indigenous communities. Because of the vastness of the material and the many cultures and nations this chapter will focus on practices of communities found on Turtle Island (North America).

The toll on health and well-being began immediately upon the arrival of Columbus in the West Indies. Diseases unknown in the hemisphere began to spread through and decimate populations across what is now North and South America and the West Indies. Policies such as the clearing of the plains and destruction of the bison herds led directly to mass starvation, which in turn, made people more susceptible to disease. These efforts at assimilation have included political, religious, economic, and medical colonialism.

While relationships during early contact in North America tended to be more reciprocal and enshrined in treaty relationships in the Canadian case, the dynamic began to shift as more settlers arrived. Government policies rapidly changed to an emphasis on assimilation which was seizing of land, relocations of peoples, outlawing of spiritual and cultural practices, and the creation of the residential school system.

This last system has had a cascade effect on families and culture that countries like Canada are just now attempting to grapple with through processes such as the Truth and Reconciliation Commission (TRC). Laws outlawing Indigenous spiritual practices in both in the United States and Canada were not repealed until the mid-20th century.

Indigenous forms of spirituality and of healing are not uniform and may vary within one nation and within families. However, all reject an atomized, individually focused approach. Instead, a sense of complete personhood includes a continual relationship with other people, culture and history, ancestors, spiritual beings, and the larger natural world. Maintaining relationships to both land and community are a prerequisite for health and this orientation is considered, "a kind of precondition for receiving that which is good in life" (Lewton and Bydone, 2000, p. 478).

Environmental racism has had a profound impact on Indigenous communities as areas on and around reserves have often been subject to the impacts of toxic substances. The deadly effluvia of oil and paper industries have directly impacted the health and well-being of Indigenous populations. Indigenous communities across North America have stood against these forces maintaining their traditional attitudes to the sacrality of land and water. For these reasons health cannot be separated from the larger projects of land claims, reparations, treaty recognition, and truth and reconciliation.

The issue of Indigenous food sovereignties also lies at the heart of health and well-being in Indigenous communities. For many access to fresh food and clean water remains an ongoing challenge. Treaty rights include the rights to traditional practices of hunting, fishing and food harvesting such as wild rice. Crawford O'Brien (2008) refers to illnesses related to diet such as type 2 diabetes as the "quintessential postcolonial disease" (10). The destruction of traditional food sources such as bison, fish, wild rice, due to extirpation and overhunting by settlers has often resulted in diets of highly processed food. Nonetheless, many First Nations have continued to practice their traditional food ways and live at least partly off the land.

Activist and writer Winona LaDuke (2016), Anishinaabegwe enrolled member of the Mississippi Band, has made reclaiming of traditional worldviews and food ways a centrepiece of her work. LaDuke has been involved in land reclamations and the restoring of sturgeon populations to the area of the White Earth Reserve in Minnesota, using stock shared by Indigenous communities in Ontario.

Similarly, the Buffalo Treaty, signed in 2014, on the Blackfeet Reserve in Montana, between numerous First Nations, has taken an active role in reintroducing wild bison back onto the prairies that encompass the Canadian and American borders. The return of the sturgeon and the bison have both religious and practical meaning and seen as restoring part of traditional life ways.

Indigenous nations developed sophisticated herbologies based on the land in which they lived. Indigenous approaches to health and healing have also included a wide knowledge of medicinal plants. These were shared with settlers and often saved their lives in the years of early contact. This worldview sees human beings as complimentary to the plant and animal nations. Medicine from within this worldview can include plants but also ritual and ceremony.

The importance of Indigenous ontologies in transforming approaches to healing are increasingly being recognized in various parts of the healthcare system. An important step taken was the founding of the Aboriginal Healing Foundation. In 1998, the government of Canada committed CAD350 million to healing initiatives for Indigenous communities across Canada. The aim was to support and initiate healing for those who were directly or indirectly harmed by their communities' experiences within the Canadian system of Indian Residential Schools.

In his book *Indigenous Healing* (2014) Ross emphasizes that there is no one size fits all approach to healing in Indigenous communities. Each community has its own history, traditions, and sacred narratives and its own struggle with colonization. Practices may include sharing in circle, going out on to the land, canoe building, berry picking and medicine gathering, sweat lodge ceremonies, and smudging.

Health concepts such as the Medicine Wheel and the idea of the Good Red Road have also developed but have been adapted by different nations in ways that work within their own communities. Increasingly these worldviews are also being shared outside of Indigenous communities in recognition of their universal value.

Many Indigenous people in both North and South America identify as Christian, and many combine together traditional practices and ceremonies with Christian practices. In turn these practices are contributing to reshaping Christianity itself by creating a more earth-centred ethos. The pilgrimage site of Lac Ste Anne in Alberta is an example of this intertwining of traditions. The waters of the lake were considered sacred to Indigenous cultures before contact and now attract Métis, Cree, Blackfoot, Dene pilgrims, some of whom are Catholic, some who blend practices, and others who practice traditional forms of spirituality.

As Indigenous people across North and South America maintain and reclaim their land and traditions the revival of spiritual and traditional practices has played a central and pivotal role.

Because ceremony has traditionally embodied law as well as custom the revival of ceremonies and rituals has been vital. Many practices, such as the Sun Dance, Sweat lodge, and Potlatch, which were forced underground have re-emerged. In other cases, new rituals and ceremonies have developed in response to contemporary challenges.

## RITUAL DRAMA AS PSYCHOTHERAPEUTIC AND HEALING CEREMONY

The Blesssingway Ceremony of the Navajo nations of the South western, US embodies core beliefs regarding healing in relation to the cosmos, community, and the individual. These rituals have been recognized as a unique form of psychotherapy. The Blessingway Ceremony understands the individual as part of a web of interrelationships that all need to be healthy. In this context health or well-being is not understood as simply having a strong body but as living within the overarching ideal of Navajo society known as *hozho na-sha* (Walking in Beauty).

From this perspective many forms of illness develop from lack of harmony and disordered relationships. This includes relationship to cultural traditions, spiritual beings, and the land. Only when this balance is in place can order and health be restored. Topper (1987) describes traditional Navajo Ceremonies as "symbolic psychotherapy" and notes that the healer will prescribe a variety of practices such as purification rites and analysis of dreams, and herbal medicines (p. 223).

In the Blessingway Ceremony, an Elder presides over the ceremony. The role of the Elders and other knowledge keepers across Turtle Island has been a vital part of the maintenance of these practices. The Navajo *haatali* (medicine man) may train for four to seven years memorizing chants and paintings, prayers religion in order to oversee these complex ceremonies.

During the ceremony the doors of the hogan, a form of traditional architecture, are locked to maintain the power and containment of the sacred space. Participants often include family and other community members. Purification rituals take place at the beginning of the practice and may consist of a number of different practices smudging with herbs like sage or sweet grass and divination rituals.

After the person being healed has been properly purified and prepared, he or she may make a confession of an action that was contrary to their cultural tradition and may include an admission of some action that has disrupted the individual's state of spiritual harmony. Each person participating is given a flint to hold as they are believed to collect the evil that is released from the individual through prayer. Flints are placed on the chest of the patient as protection.

The room is then darkened and the *haatali* begins the prayer in which the individual is identified with a heroic mythological ancestor often by lying on a sand painting. This process is meant to bring the patient into direct relationship with the Holy People and he or she may lie directly on a sand painting of these ancestors.

At the end of the prayer the evil held in the flints is symbolically released and sent to a remote location in "the North" where it is rendered harmless. The final ritual is the offering of corn pollen which is placed on the sand painting. With this the relationship between the healer, the patient, the Holy People, and the symbols is completed. The patient then stays on the site and rests for four days.

This ceremony is understood as being rooted in, and related to, the sacrality of a place between the four sacred mountains. These practices are grounded in a specific place and history emphasizing connections to ancestors, community and family. This recognition that places cannot simply be substituted for another is central to Indigenous worldviews and that each place is specific, and the rituals and beliefs are directly linked to them.

## *Walking in Beauty: Closing Prayer from the Navajo Way Blessing Ceremony*

In beauty I walk
With beauty before me I walk
With beauty behind me I walk
With beauty above me I walk
With beauty around me I walk
It has become beauty again
Hózhóogo naasháa doo
Shitsijí' hózhóogo naasháa doo

Shikéédéé hózhóogo naasháa doo
Shideigi hózhóogo naasháa doo
T'áá altso shinaagóó hózhóogo naasháa doo
Hózhó náhásdlíí'
Hózhó náhásdlíí'
Hózhó náhásdlíí'
Hózhó náhásdlíí'
Today I will walk out, today everything negative will leave me.
I will be as I was before, I will have a cool breeze over my body.
I will have a light body, I will be happy forever, nothing will hinder me.
I walk with beauty before me. I walk with beauty behind me.
I walk with beauty below me. I walk with beauty above me.
I walk with beauty around me. My words will be beautiful.
In beauty all day long may I walk.
Through the returning seasons may I walk.
On the trail marked with pollen may I walk.
With dew about my feet may I walk.
With beauty before me may I walk.
With beauty behind me may I walk.
With beauty below me may I walk.
With beauty above me may I walk.
With beauty all around me may I walk.
In old age wandering on a trail of beauty, lively, may I walk.
In old age wandering on a trail of beauty, living again, may I walk.
My words will be beautiful…

—Yale Forum on Religion and Ecology, Sacred Texts, https://fore.yale.edu/World-Religions/Indigenous/Misc/Sacred-Texts

## THE POWWOW AND JINGLE DRESS: COMMUNITY REVITALIZATION, ART, CEREMONY, AND HEALING

Powwows are ceremonies that showcase Indigenous music, dances, regalia, food and art. Commonly hosted by First Nations, Metis, or Inuit communities they may be either on reserve or in urban settings or may be hosted by educational institutions such as universities and colleges. Since the 1950s, powwows have been growing in size, number and popularity welcoming both Indigenous and non-Indigenous audiences across Turtle Island.

The physical setting of the powwow expresses an Indigenous cosmology and typically involves a series of concentric circles with the drums and musicians located at the centre. The ceremony often takes place outdoors. with the drum representing connection to the heartbeat of Mother Earth.

Regalia plays an important role in reclaiming identity and culture within the setting of the powwow. Ceremonial outfits are often intricately beaded and colours used may indicate ties to family and clan and are specific to the individual. The evolving nature of the regalia, like the ritual, itself reflects the individual and children may choose to have the symbol of a super hero along with the more traditional porcupine quills or eagle feathers.

These ceremonies have played a vital role in sharing knowledge of culture that may have been lost, reinforcing practices and in educating children and the larger public. Powwows are now common in communities across Canada and the US in a variety of settings. Emerging from traditional ceremonies they now play an evolving role as a space of cultural, political, and spiritual resurgence.

A common sight at powwows in northern Ontario and north east US is a group of women wearing dresses that create the sound of jingling bells or cones called *ziibaaska'iganan*. A whole worldview and attitude towards healing can be understood through this garment and practice of the healing ceremony.

The origin story for the Jingle Dance ritual varies but all place its origins within the Ojibway/Anishinaabeg culture that spans the Canadian/American border and takes in Wisconsin, Minnesota, and Ontario. The most common origin story states that around 1917 a young girl was dangerously ill (perhaps from Spanish Influenza) and her father sought help through dream and vision. He was granted a vision/dream of the dress and instructed that the girl was to wear it and take "sprightly steps".

In all versions the association of the dress with healing is emphasized. This ritual healing practice illustrates the way that dance, aesthetics, and spirituality contribute to overall well-being. The regalia of the jingle dress is prepared over the course of a year with prayers over every bell that is sewn onto the garment.

The practice of healing through the dances associated with the jingle dress demonstrates the ways in which new ceremonies have developed based on traditional epistemologies The jingle dress ceremony maintains the centrality of vision, aesthetics, music, and dance. Emerging as they do from dream and vision these ritual performances are flexible enough to address themselves to changing times and circumstances.

## MIYUPIMAATISIIUN "BEING ALIVE WELL": CREE CONCEPTS OF HEALTH

The Eastern Cree who live 1400 km north of Montreal, Quebec have undertaken a challenging journey to wrest back control over their well-being. Facing the influences of traders, missionaries, and the threat of a hydro-electric dam projects that would have flooded vast tracts of their territory. Their fight against damage to the land is directly related to Cree ideas of health which are based in a respectful and spiritual relationship to land and animal relations.

As part of their agreement with the Canadian and Quebec governments the community now has control over both education and health. Land sovereignty is also related to food sovereignty which are central to Cree beliefs about health and well-being. To be able to partake of traditional food is a vital aspect of "being alive well". The importing of unhealthy processed food has had detrimental impacts on health in many Northern communities.

Sovereignty has allowed for the reassertion of traditional viewpoints that place relationship to the land at the centre, asking the question, "If the land is not healthy then how can we be?" Cree understanding of health points to the ways in which well-being is directly connected to political autonomy. This, in turn, is connected to control of education and health care as well as food sovereignty, and language and land protection. Nothing of these aspects can be separated from one another and are encapsulated in the word *miyupimaatisiiun*.

### The Hollow Tree: A Case Study in Recovery

The personal narrative of Herb Nabigon in his book *The Hollow Tree: Fighting Addiction with Traditional Native Healing* (2006) offers an insider perspective on how the return to traditional practices fosters healing. Nabigon was born into an Anishinaabeg Ojibway family in Pic Mobert, Northern Ontario. His father lived a traditional life hunting and trapping in the bush, and he says, "He was a man of strong spirit and was very close to nature" (4).

Nabigon was sent to a residential school as part of Canadian government policy at age nine. As he notes, in the 1950s fasting and sweat lodge ceremonies were forbidden on his reserve. He was sent to school far from his home where he was stripped of his identity including his name and language.

Nabigon attended university and began a job in the government but the ongoing impacts of trauma and dislocation from his community led to an increasing problem with alcohol. However, issues came to a head as his marriage ended and he was informed by his employer that he would either have to get his drinking under control or lose his job.

This was a turning point in Nabigon's life as it brought him back into contact with traditional practices. This began what he referred to as the Long Road Home when he entered a 12-step programme that also used First Nations paradigms of healing in Alberta. Nabigon (2006) was told by his spiritual teacher, "You can either pick up your sacred bundle or you can die from drinking" (p. 33).

Nabigon attributed much of his success in turning his life around to the influence of the Elders who ran the programme. He benefited from teachings in Indigenous philosophy and psychology all of which is based upon a spiritual understanding. In looking back on the impact of these systems of healing Napigon writes that, "I think the most valuable gift the Elders gave me was teaching me how to pray" (p. 35).

In the final half of the book Nabigon offers these teachings to all saying that that these philosophies can contribute to a state of inner harmony and better personal relationships for everyone regardless of their cultural background. Nabigon makes it clear that spiritual philosophy is to be lived and not just thought about and throughout the rest of his life he was politically active around issues such as land claims. His religious beliefs and their role in his healing are central to his narrative. Napigon concludes that western society has become hollow and without substance and it is "only with these beliefs can the hollow tree be transformed into a sacred tree it was meant to be" (vii).

"I am grateful today, I'm thankful to have spent quality time with the Elders, whose spirit world was gracious enough to guide me. It was through their example and care that I was able to receive the traditional teachings and learn how to use them for my own benefit.

It has been a good journey for me. My struggle for the relighting of my personal power has been a tough road, but I wouldn't have it any other way. My new-found power has helped me to open up my mind and to understand my feelings. It has certainly helped me with my spiritual development and it is all because of the Elders' patience and belief in me. Their perseverance and strength to preserve our spiritual beliefs and fight for me is moving. I am forever grateful for the Elders" (Napigon, 2006, pp. 103–4).

## *The Medicine Wheel*

The medicine wheel has been taught in a variety of ways depending on the knowledge keeper. But in all cases the holistic nature of the teaching can be seen in the understanding of the many dimensions of the human person. These, in turn, are situated in the connect of relationship to kin—both human and non-human persons, and to the Earth.

—Kaaren Dannenmann, Trout Lake, Medicine Wheel Teaching: https://www.youtube.com/watch?v=oGC1EncFa50

## REFLECTION

1. Write down and reflect on your state of health in each of these quadrants of physical body, mind, emotions and spirit. It is important to be scrupulously honest in undertaking this practice.
2. What could you do to strengthen those aspects that are in need of attention?
3. What is the current state of your relationship with the land you live on and all our relations (animals, plants, water)? If you are in North America- do you know what Treaty you are living on?
4. What are the threats to the eco-system in which you live?

## REFERENCES


Crawford O'Brien, Suzanne J. (2008). "Introduction." *Religion and Healing in Native America. Pathways for Renewal*. Suzanne J. Crawford O'Brien (Ed.). Praeger.

LaDuke, Winona. (2016). *Recovering the Sacred. The Importance of Naming and Claiming*. Haymarket Books.

Nabigon, Herb. (2006). *The Hollow Tree: Fighting Addiction with Traditional Native Healing*. McGill-Queen's University Press.

Lewton, Elizabeth C. and Victoria Bydone (2000). "Identity and Healing in Three Navajo Religious Traditions: Sa'ah Naaghai Bik'eh Hozho," *Medical Anthropology Quarterly*, 14 (4), 476–497.

Ross, Rupert. (2014). *Indigenous Healing. Exploring Traditional Paths*. Penguin Books.

Topper, Martin D. (1987). The Traditional Navajo Medicine Man: Therapist, Counselor, and Community Leader. *Journal of Psychoanalytic Anthropology*, 10 (3), 217–249.

Truth and Reconciliation Commission, https://rcaanc-cirnac.gc.ca/eng/1450124405592/1529106060525


## FURTHER READING


Adelson, Naomi. (2000). *Being Alive Well: Health and the Politics of Cree Well-Being*. The University of Toronto Press.

Brown, Matthew. (2014). Bison Treaty Signed by Alberta, Montana, Tribes. CBC, September 23, 2014. https://www.cbc.ca/news/canada/calgary/bison-treaty-signed-by-alberta-montana-tribes-1.2775965

Browner, Tara. (2002). *Heartbeat of the People. Music and Dance of the Northern Pow-Wow*. University of Illinois Press.

Daschuk, James. (2013). *Clearing the Plains: Disease, Politics of Starvation and Loss of Aboriginal Life*. University of Regina Press.

DeLisle, Raina. (2021). This is Where Canada Dumps Tons of Toxic Waste, Tailing Ponds-and Racism. *Chatelaine*, March 19, 2021.

Frost, Asha. (2022). *You Are The Medicine: 13 Moons of Indigenous Wisdom, Ancestral Connection, and Animal Spirit Guidance*. Hay House Inc.

Gone, Joseph. (2003). Indian Mental Health Service Delivery: Persistent Challenges. *Culturally Diverse Mental Health: The Challenges of*

*Research and Resistance*. Jeffrey Scott Mio and Gayle Y. Iwamasa (Eds.). Brunner-Routledge.

Johnston, Basil. (2008). *Ojibway Heritage*. McLelland & Stewart. Originally published in 1976.

Kelm, Mary Ellen. (1998). *Colonizing Bodies. Aboriginal Health and Healing In British Columbia 1900–50*. UBC Press.

Kimmerer, Robin Wall. (2013). *Braiding Sweetgrass. Indigenous Wisdom, Scientific Knowledge and the Teachings of Plants*. Milkweed Editions.

LaDuke, Winona. (2020). *To Be a Water Protector: The Rise of the Wiindigoo Slayers*. Fernwood Publishing.

Manjeshwar, Sanjana. (2021). The Lasting Harms of Toxic Exposure in Native American Communities. *Berkeley Political Review*, July 10, 2021.

Martin-Hill, Dawn. (2010). Women in Indigenous Traditions. *Women And Religious Traditi*ons. Leona M. Anderson and Pamela Dickey Young (Eds.). Oxford University Press.

Miller, Heather Andrew. Regalia Evolves With the Dancer. *Windspeaker*. Archived 2006. https://windspeaker.com/node/events/9189

Palmateer, Pamela. (2020). *Warrior Life. Indigenous Resistance and Resurgence*. Fernwood Publishing.

Peltier, Cindy. (2021). Indigenous Conceptions of Living Well. In R. Schiff and H. Møller (Eds.), *Health and Health Care in Northern Canada*. University of Toronto Press.

Skye, Courtney (2022). Food is How We Heal. *Chatelaine*. September 2022.

Spear, Wayne K. (2014). *Full Circle. The Aboriginal Healing Foundation And the Unfinished Work of Hope, Healing and Reconciliation*. Aboriginal Healing Foundation.

Thiesz, R.D. (2005). Putting Things in Order. The Discourse of Tradition. *Powwow*. Clyde Ellis, Luke Eric Lassister, and Gary H Dunham. University of Nebraska Press.

Waldron, Ingrid G. (2018). *There's Something in the Water: Environmental Racism in Indigenous and Black Communities*. Fernwood Publishing.

Wiremu, Nia, Allister Bush, and David Epston. (2017). *Collaborative And Indigenous Mental Health Therapy: Tataihoho, Stories of Maori Healing and Psychiatry*. Routledge.

## INTERNET RESOURCES

Biinaagami: Our Shared Responsibility to the Great Lakes. https://www.biinaagami.org/

Cottagers and Indians, CBC doc POV, July 3, 2020. https://www.cbc.ca/cbcdocspov/episodes/cottagers-indians

Four Directions Teachings. Produced by National Indigenous Literacy Association, Canadian Heritage. https://fourdirectionsteachings.com/

Medicine in Your Backyard. How Indigenous Peoples Have Used Medicinal Plants. Courtney Markewich, CBC News, posted August 5, 2017. https://www.cbc.ca/news/canada/saskatoon/indigenous-medicinal-walk-1.4235900

Native People's Concepts of Health and Illness. Native Voices. https://www.nlm.nih.gov/nativevoices/exhibition/healing-ways/medicine-ways/introduction.html

Origins of Women's Jingle Dress Dancing. Indian Country Today. Originally published January 28, 2011, updated September 13, 2018. https://indiancountrytoday.com/archive/origins-of-womens-jingle-dress-dancing

The Aboriginal Healing Foundation, archived records. https://www.ahf.ca/

Walk in Beauty. The Purpose of Life. https://www.youtube.com/watch?v=EP4_lDph2io

The United Nations Declaration on the Rights of Indigenous Peoples. https://www.ohchr.org/en/indigenous-peoples/un-declaration-rights-indigenous-peoples

# 5 The Art of Living: Hinduism and Healing

Hinduism is the term used to describe the many traditions that developed over thousands of years in the Indian sub-continent. It is impossible to reduce Hinduism to a set of simplified ideas and variety is the hallmark of the tradition. Typically, five duties are recognized by most Hindus, to live virtuously, or according to dharma, to worship appropriately (*utsava*), to honour the rites of passage (*samskaras*) and to go on pilgrimage (*tirthayatra*).

Hindus may practice rites for their ancestors, reverence of the natural world, and devotional rituals. They may engage in highly abstract philosophy and aesthetics and believe in many gods, one or none. The divine may be imagined as the ground of being, male, female, or androgynous.

Dharma is a central concept that refers to moral, religious, and social duties and these have traditionally been shaped by caste, gender, and stage of life. Because dharma is so nuanced the great epics of the tradition the *Ramayana* and the *Mahabharata* are centrally concerned with determining correct moral and dharmic action. These sacred narratives have been so influential they will be known by almost anyone living in India regardless of their cultural background.

The other important stream within the larger Hindu tradition is that followed by the renunciant—the person who leaves the usual social world and focuses on spiritual liberation (*moksha*). This quest is treated with great respect within Hindu culture and is seen as the path of greatest intensity and efficacy for gaining release from the cycle of birth, death, and rebirth.

Philosophers and thinkers on the ascetic path have shaped the ideas and ideals of schools of thought such as yoga and Advaita Vedanta. These thinkers developed the complex philosophies of karma—the idea that one's actions, thoughts, and speech influence both ones current life and future rebirths.

**DOI: 10.4324/9781003471769-5**

The Hindu tradition accepts that there are various paths towards the ultimate goal of spiritual liberation. These are sometimes grouped together as the path of wisdom, the path of works, and the path of devotion. However, this can make things seem too tidy and many combine aspects of varying approaches.

## HEALING AND HEALING IN THE HINDU TRADITION

Developing as it has over thousands of years and in many regions of the sub-continent there is a rich and varied approach to healing in the Hindu tradition. Concepts of the etiology of disease also take in a wide variety of ideas and approaches from naturalistic to spiritual. Practical and physically based interventions such as pulse diagnosis and surgery have always existed alongside a vast pharmacopoeia and spiritual interventions such as the practice of prayer and mantra.

The quest for health and healing appears prominently in the Vedas, the oldest written scripture. In the *Rig Veda* the central aim is to maintain alignment with *rta*, the sacred order. This connection with higher law was meant to ensure that relationships to the ancestors, community, divine and the natural world were maintained and to allow for well-being.

The seeking of an auspicious and blessed life remains the ideal in the Hindu tradition. Good health, from this point of view, is understood as being necessary to pursuing higher goals of spiritual liberation and from this perspective "health seeking was a religious obligation" (Desai, 2012, p. 40).

The traditional ideal of good health is expressed in the wish to live a long life. In a hymn to Rudra, the unpredictable and powerful storm God, the verse goes as follows:

> By those most healing medicines that you give Rudra, I would attain a hundred winters. Drive hatred away from me, and anguish farther away; drive diseases away in all directions … Raise up our heroes with your healing medicines; I hear that of all healers you are the best.
>
> *(RG 2.33 2-4)*

These recitations demonstrate the intertwining of the divine with all aspects of health and healing and general good fortune.

Healing mantras appear in both the *Rig Veda* and *Artharva Veda* and focus on a variety of concerns including general health, fertility, and freedom from disease. From the beginning the tradition developed a vast pharmacopeia. The sacrality of these medicines is seen in a hymn directly addressed to the sacred and healing nature of plants stating:

> The tawny plants were born in ancient times, three ages before the gods; now I will meditate on their hundred and seven forms. Mothers, you have a hundred forms and a thousand growths You who have a hundred ways of working, make this man whole for me.
>
> *(RG 10.97-1-4)*

These plants, especially those used in healing, are considered to be sacred and are to be treated with reverence. Knowledge of healing plants remains part of the training of traditional Hindu healers and practitioners of Ayurveda. A reverence and recognition of the sacredness of nature, including animals and the larger environment, is central to the Hindu tradition.

The figure of the healer and doctor appear in these earliest Hindu texts alongside the belief that healing and healers are directly connected to the divine. The Ashvins, the twin sons of the Surya the sun God, are depicted as divine physicians who rescue people from disaster. The Ashvins are praised for "bringing wealth with good kingship, long life blessed with fine children and true heroism "(RG 1.119). From this point of view physical health and well-being are not separated from good fortune and a well lived life.

## ATTITUDES TO SUFFERING IN THE HINDU TRADITION

Hinduism developed various understanding related to suffering of which illness is simply one form. From this point of view illness can result from purely environmental and natural sources such as poor diet or from complex out workings of the laws of karma. The Samkhya-yoga tradition, one of the orthodox schools (*darshanas*), states that there are three categories of suffering: self-inflicted (*adhyatmika duhkha*), arising from the actions of others (*adibhautika duhkha*), and "acts of God(s)" (*adhdaivika duhkha*).

The first form of suffering arises from one's own body/mind and can be physical, emotional, or mental. This type of pain is the most amenable to change and can be addressed in a wide variety of ways including changes in life-style, diet, use of prayers, mantra, meditation. The second form of suffering recognizes that the decisions and actions of others may have profound impacts on our well-being and harmonizing personal relationships then is an important part of managing this form of suffering.

The third category of suffering includes events such as earthquakes, floods, and epidemics. These are viewed as being part of destiny and may be understood as resulting from powers outside of human control. The appropriate response to these sorts of problems is through prayer and seeking out various forms of protection.

Another important perspective on suffering developed within the Hindu tradition is the idea that challenges are part of the process of spiritual awakening. This is illustrated in the section of the *Bhagavad Gita* called "The Vishad of Arjuna" when the great warrior Arjuna is driven to his knees by despair and confusion regarding how to fulfill his duty in life without harming others. It is only in this state of profound humility that he is given the divine eye by the God Krishna and is able to see the truth and take action.

Sacred narratives such as these demonstrate the idea that human growth is often brought about by situations of pain and suffering. These may result in the breaking down of personal ego and allow for a state of openness in which spiritual insights can enter. And, in fact, from this point of view a life that is too easy may result in very little development.

## THE LAWS OF KARMA AND HEALTH

The Hindu tradition, and many of the spiritual paths that emerge from South Asia, such as Jainism and Buddhism, share the belief in the doctrine of karma. This philosophy is based on a belief in reincarnation and the law of cause and effect that works across lifetimes.

The Upanishads, written circa 600 BCE, offer the first clear outline of karma theory in the Hindu tradition. The texts describe the destiny of the soul (*atman*) that is reincarnated again and again according to the laws of karma. The only way to escape from the endless cycle of birth and rebirth is to attain the state of liberation (*moksha*).

While these theories are extremely complex there is a general understanding that karma impacts upon health. There are fixed karmas such where a person is born, their general constitution and family of origin. From this point of view the broader parameters of one's life are determined by actions in previous lives that play out in the present and into the future.

However, there are also ways in which less fixed karmas can be impacted. This generally includes practices such as prayer, mantra after consultation with a *pandit* (priest) or other religious specialists. It is common for the *pandit*, to consult the person's horoscope and to prescribe a variety of practices (*upayas*) to help mitigate and improve the person's circumstances. These can include giving to charity, volunteering/selfless service (*seva*), wearing specific gemstones, performing acts of kindness to other people or animals. These practices are typically performed alongside other therapies including consulting a physician.

## LORD DHANVANTARI: DIVINE PARADIGM OF THE HEALER

The Hindu tradition developed the ideal of the Divine Doctor embodied in the figure of Lord Dhanvantari, the God of Medicine. He is believed to be an incarnation of God Vishnu and the originator of Ayurveda. The origins of Lord Dhanvantari are found in a variety of myths about his birth.

According to one of the sacred narrative Indra, the king of the Devatas, was once cursed with being bereft of all strength, energy, and good fortune. As a result of this curse, *asuras* (demons) led by king Bali, defeated Indra and took control of the universe.

In response to this disaster that resulted in the overturning of the proper world order, Indra and other *devas* went to Lord Vishnu for help. Lord Vishnu advised them to treat the *asuras* in a diplomatic manner. As a result, the Devas formed an alliance with asuras to jointly churn the ocean in order to attain the nectar of immortality (*amrita*). During the churning of the cosmic ocean, many divine objects and beings emerged. At the end of this process, Lord Dhanvantari appeared from the ocean carrying with him a pot filled with the divine nectar of immortality.

According to the narrative, after Lord Indra had witnessed many people afflicted by pain and disease he pleaded with Lord Dhanvantari to descend into the material world and teach Ayurveda to the human race. As a result, Lord Dhanvantari was born into the royal household of Kashi and eventually became king. Even as a young boy he had ascetic tendencies, was extremely disciplined and performed severe austerities. He then went on to teach Ayurveda orally to the sages and those who became his disciples. His teachings are believed to be recorded in the *Agni Purana*, as well as being passed through the teachings of his disciples.

The *Srimad Bhagavatam* 17.4 states that, "One who remembers the name of Dhanvantari can be released from all disease". Rituals are performed to Dhanvantari two days before Diwali, the Festival of Lights. At dusk, a lamp pointing toward North-East is lit at the doorstep of the house to welcome Lord Dhanvantari for health and happiness in life. It is believed that Lord Dhanvantari destroys negativity and blesses his devotees with happiness, prosperity and good health.

## RELIGIOUS THERAPEUTICS IN HINDUISM

Many of religio-philosophical schools of Hinduism like yoga, were developed with spiritual rather than physical ends in mind. However, physical and mental health are generally understood as being a necessary aspect of spiritual life. As a result, care and preparation of the physical body is an important component of practice. The body is then a vehicle for reaching enlightenment.

The idea that there is an eternal divine core (*atman*) in all people is common to all the orthodox Hindu traditions. However, the various schools have developed a wide variety of methodologies for accessing it. According to hatha yoga pioneer B. K. S. Iyengar (2005) the body is the doorway to Higher Reality. He writes, "Health begins with firmness in body, deepens to emotional stability, then leads to intellectual clarity, wisdom and finally the unveiling of the soul" (23).

Yoga is one of the six orthodox systems within the Hindu tradition and was systemized by the sage Patanjali circa 100–500 CE. The eight limbs of yoga offer a variety of physical and psycho-spiritual practices aimed at achieving liberation. The limbs include ethical conduct, physical postures, self-reflective study, and deepening forms of concentration and meditation. The limbs are a holistic system for cleansing and purifying all aspects of the self and leading ultimately to enlightenment/liberation (*samadhi*).

The first limbs of yoga are dedicated to purifying and stabilizing the body and mind. The tradition recognizes that a disordered mind and disordered emotions as the source of illusion and misguided action. Purification is brought about by proper diet, life routines, prayer and self-reflection and receiving of teachings. The final limbs emphasize the journey inward and focus on working with breath and more and more concentrated forms of meditation.

## THE SUBTLE BODY

Generally in Hinduism the body is understood as being an energy system. In the Upanishads a model emerges of the body as a system that moves from being a dense physical body (*annamaya kosha*) to the most subtle (*anandamaya kosha*). This body-mind is understood as being dynamic rather than a static entity but is set within a web of karmic processes.

The chakra system built on these ideas with energy centres contributing to the ascension of consciousness. Some traditional sources describe five or seven chakras and others eight. The chakras are often described as being aligned in an ascending column from the base of the spine to the top of the head. Typically, each chakra is associated with a certain colour and sound, seed syllable and symbol. The ascension up the spine represents the ascension of consciousness from the material to the subtle and finally the transcendent.

It is believed that the chakras vitalize the physical body and influence the physical, emotional and mental aspects of the mind and body. They are considered to be the loci of life-energy usually referred to as *prana*. The main function of the chakras is to draw in the *prana* by spinning around their own axes and hold it in their respective sphere to maintain and balance the spiritual, mental, emotional, and physical well-being of the mind and body.

The body is often depicted as being energized by a system of *nadis* that carry subtle energy (*prana*) throughout the body. These are believed to function as a sort of energy grid that functions optimally when energy is unobstructed. For this reason, a wide variety of healing techniques may be used in order to ensure the smooth flow of energy. These may include *pranayama*, working with sound through chanting or music, various physical postures (*asana*), and massage.

## AYURVEDA: WISDOM FOR LIFE

The Ayurvedic system emerged from the earliest Hindu scripture developing over thousands of years. The Ayurvedic medical corpus remains in use into the present with the most influential texts being the *Charaka Samhita*, the *Sushruta Samhita* and *Ashtanga Samgraha*.

Ayurveda emphasizes the importance of the person's constitution in relation to the environment.

The *Charaka Samhita* includes an introduction to health, medicine, hygiene, prophylactics, diet and lifestyle. The work includes an extensive pharmacopeia. This work was translated into Arabic and Persian, and its influence extended into the western world through the Latin translation of Razes and Avicenna.

The eight disciplines of Ayurveda rendered in modern terms are 1. General Medicine; 2. Paediatrics; 3. Psychiatry; 4. Ear, Nose, and Throat; 5, Surgery; 6. Toxicology; 7. Geriatrics; and 8. Reproductive Medicine. These disciplines were taught either through the traditional *guru parampara* or in the ancient universities of India such as Taxila. The teaching of Ayurveda at the Buddhist Nalanda University demonstrates the joint influences of Hinduism and Buddhism on these medical practices (Rhymer, 2017, p. 13).

The Ayurvedic tradition encompasses science, religion and philosophy (Lad, 2019, p. 15). While recognizing that individuals are born with strengths and weaknesses the system aims at a vital and energized body and clear and conscious mind. From an Ayurvedic perspective there is no split between the body and mind and each influences the other.

Ayurveda is also concerned with the larger context of healing and traces back many diseases to the environment and to the impacts of changes of season. This approach is embedded within a larger South Asian worldview emphasizing personal hygiene, daily discipline, rituals, and contemplation.

Life in the world is also conditioned by the three qualities of *sattva, rajas*, and *tamas*, the qualities of clearness, lightness, activity and inertia, respectively. According to the Ayurvedic model each person is born with a certain constitution (*dosha*) which is a mixture of vata, pitta, kapha each of which has its own intrinsic strengths and weaknesses that need to be worked with.

According to the physician-scholar Charaka, the doctor was to gain a broad education including knowledge of anatomy, the course of diseases and pharmacology. Charaka also had harsh words for any practitioner who was not practicing ethically. Despite the need for extensive education in diseases and their treatment, according to Charaka, compassion had to be the basis of the actions of a doctor.

An Ayurvedic *vaid* (physician) can discern a person's constitution by observation. Appointments generally consist of pulse diagnosis, and examination of the tongue and eyes. The physician will also typically enquire about lifestyle and stress levels. The overall approach is based on preventative medicine so a great deal of emphasis is placed on habits such as proper sleep and a healthy diet. Ayurveda also has a focus on rejuvenation practices and medications that build up the *ojas* (well-being, immunity) of the body if it has been depleted by disease, exhaustion, or stress.

## HINDUISM AND HEALING IN THE CONTEMPORARY WORLD

Ayurveda has evolved over time and has been reconfigured in its negotiations with colonialism and modernity and continues to be an intrinsic part of the system of health care in India. Ayurvedic clinics, hospitals, dispensaries can be found across the subcontinent. Teaching may occur within the guru system in the university system or a combination of the two. As a result of the diaspora Ayurvedic medicine has now become available in countries around the world and increasingly to a public that is attracted to holistic forms of health and healing.

Vasant Lad (Lad, 2002) was one of the first to bring the practice and teaching of Ayurveda to North America. Before moving to the United States, he was Medical Director of the Ayurveda Hospital in Pune, India and Professor of Clinical Medicine at the Pune University College of Ayurvedic Medicine.

In 1984 he founded the Ayurvedic Institute in Albuquerque, New Mexico. The institute, which has since moved to Ashville, North Carolina, offers: training for Ayurvedic counsellors, practitioners, and doctors, treatments and also houses a clinic, library, and Ayurvedic Press. Lad has published extensively on the topic of Ayurveda, understanding it as a universally effective healing system. He writes that, "To understand Ayurveda is to understand the forces that engender our well being as well as those that lie at the root of disease" (Lad, 2019, p. 151).

The yoga tradition has continued to have deep and enduring impacts on Hindu and western approaches to health, both physical and mental. A growing body of research is making yoga's insights and practices available to those who work in all areas of health care. The teaching of yoga has become a resource for psychologists and psychotherapists with the growing recognition that experiences are retained in the body as well as in the mind.

Amy Weintraub (2004) has worked with yoga and trauma noting that negative memories are often held in the body and breath and so working with them requires a variety of techniques. There are increasing numbers of therapists who practice integrative psychotherapy that includes practices such as meditation, postures, and guided visualization (p. 33).

Dean Ornish, an American medical doctor has made newspaper headlines and written best-selling books discussing the ways in which yoga can be brought into western health care. His work is in reversing heart disease through the combination of vegetarian diet, psychotherapy, and yogic techniques such asana and breath work and meditation.

Ornish studied with Hindu guru Swami Satchiananda and recognized the challenges involved in bringing the teaching into mainstream discourse. Ornish carefully reframed the teachings in language that fit more easily within the secular medical paradigm.

Ornish has emphasized the need for holistic practices rejecting the typical "magic bullet" approach touted by so much of western health care. As a result of many successes the insights of Hindu therapeutics are now making their way into the tool kits of physicians and psychologists. The clinically proven efficacy of Ornish's programme has resulted it now being covered by Medicare in the United States.

## REFLECTIONS

1. Why do you think holistic systems like Yoga and Ayurveda have become so popular in the western world?
2. How would understanding the human body as energy impact attitudes to and practices of healing?
3. Take the online Ayurvedic quiz.

## OVERVIEW OF HINDUISM

There are an estimated 950 million to a billion Hindus around the world. The majority of Hindus live in India and there are large Hindu populations in the West Indies, Canada, the US, and the UK and western Europe.

There is no founder of the Hindu tradition, the *rsis* (sages) were believed to have heard the first revelations recorded in the Vedas.

Main Divisions: Vaishavite (followers of Vishnu), Shaivite (Shiva), Shakta (the Goddess)

Holy City: Varanasi (Benares)

Scriptural Language: Sanskrit

Texts: Hinduism possesses many sacred texts and these vary from region to region. The Vedas are generally considered to be sacred by all Hindus and other important texts include: *The Ramayana*, the *Mahabharata*, including the *Bhagavad Gita* and the *Puranas*.

Religious Specialists: authority rests in variety of places. Traditionally the Brahmin, priestly caste, has been responsible for temple-based rituals and teachings. Many renounced ascetics hold spiritual power as do gurus (spiritual teachers).

## DEATH AND THE AFTERLIFE

Hindus believe in reincarnation and that the *atman* (soul) is reincarnated in various forms until it finally achieves *moksha* (liberation). Hindus generally practice cremation. Typically, ashes are sprinkled in a body of water with sacred rivers such as the Ganges being preferred sites.

## REFERENCES

Desai, Prakash N. (2012). Indian Religion and the Ayurvedic Tradition. *Oxford Textbook of Spirituality in Health Care*. Mark Cobb, Christina M. Puchalski, and Bruce Rumbold (Eds). Oxford University Press.

Iyengar, B. K. S. (2005). *Light on Life. The Yoga Journey to Wholeness, Inner Peace and Ultimate Freedom*. Raincoast Books.

Lad, Vasant. (2002). *Textbook of Ayurveda Volume One. The Fundamental Principles*. The Ayurvedic Press.

Ornish, Dean. (1990). *Dr. Dean Ornish's Program for Reversing Heart Disease*. Bantam Books.

Rhymer, Hans H. (2017). *Llewelleyns Complete Book of Ayurveda*. Llewelleyn Publishers.

Weintraub, Amy. (2004). *Yoga for Depression: A Compassionate Guide to Relieve Suffering Through Yoga*. Broadway Books.

## FURTHER READING

*Ayurveda, The Art of Being*. (2001). Dir. Pan Nalin.

Basham, A. L. (1976). The Practice of Medicine in Ancient and Medieval India. *Asian Medical Systems: A Comparative Study*. Charles M. Leslie (Ed.). University of California Press.

Berger, Rachel. (2013). *Ayurveda Made Modern. Political Histories of Indigenous Medicine in Northern India, 1900–1955*. Palgrave Macmillan.

Bhide, S. R., Bhargav, H., Gangaddhar B. N., and Desai G. (2023). Exploring the Therapeutic Potential of Yoga Philosophy: A Perspective on the Need for Yoga-Based Counseling Program (YBCP) in Common Mental Disorders. *Indian Journal of Psychological Medicine*, 45 (4), 420–29.

Bodecker, G. and Burford, G. (Eds.). (2007). *Traditional, Complimentary and Alternative Medicine. Policy and Public Health Perspectives*. Imperial College Press.

Chakrabarti, Pratik. (2014). *Medicine and Empire. 1600–1960*. Palgrave Macmillan.

Charaka. (2017). *Charaka Samhita*. Shashirekha H. K. and Bargale Sushant Sukumar (Eds.). Chaukhambha Publications.

Davis, Lauren, Alexandra Aylward, and Rebecca Buchanan. (Jul/Aug 2022). Trauma Informed Yoga: Investigating and Intervention for Mitigating Adverse Childhood Experiences in Rural Settings. *Educational Studies*, 58 (4), 530–59.

*Dhavantari-Nighantu*. (2008). Translated by Amritpal Singh. Chaukhamba Orientalia.

Fields, Gregory P. (2001). *Religious Therapeutics. Body and Health in Yoga, Ayurveda, and Tantra*. Motilal Benarsidass.

Glazier, A., Colin Blackmore, and Sheila Jennett. (2001). Hinduism and The Body. *The Oxford Companion to the Body*. Oxford University Press.

Joshi, Vinod Kumar, Apurva Joshi, and Kartar Singh Dhiman. (2017). The Ayurvedic Pharmacopoeia of India, Development and Perspectives. *Journal of Ethnopharmacology*, 197, 32–8.

Katiyar, C. K. and Pulok K. Mukherjee. (2017). Some Excerpts from Charaka Samhita—An Ancient Treatise on Ayurveda and Healthy Living. *Journal of Ethnopharmacology*, 197, 3–9.

Lad, Vasant. *Textbook of Ayurveda. Volume Two. A Complete Guide to Clinical Assessment*. The Ayurvedic Press.

Lad, Vasant. *Textbook of Ayurveda. Volume Three. General Principles of Management and Treatment*. The Ayurvedic Press.

Lad, Vasant. (2019). *Ayurveda. The Science of Self-Healing*. Lotus Press. Originally published in 1984.

Loukas, Marios, Alexis Lanteri, Julie Ferrauiola R. Shane Tubbs, Goppi Maharaja, Mohammadali Mohajel Shoja, Abishek Yadav, and Vishnu Chellapilla Rao. (2010). Anatomy in Ancient India: A Focus on the Susruta Samhita. *Journal of Anatomy*, 217 (6), 646–50.

Patwardhan, Kishor. (2012). The History of the Discovery of Blood Circulation: Unrecognized Contributions of Ayurvedic Masters. *Advances in Physiology Education*, 36 (2), 77–82.

Raveenthiran, Venkatachalam. (2011). Knowledge of Ancient Hindu Surgeons on Hirschsprung Disease: Evidence from Sushruta Samhita of circa 1200–600 BC. *Journal of Pediatric Surgery*, 46 (11), 2204–8.

Sharma, Pundit S. (Ed). (1979). *Realms of Ayurveda*. Arnold-Heinemann.

Sreekuman, T Nagendra and Havarasu, J. (2020). Mindfulness and Yoga: A Parallel and Comparative Analysis. *International Journal of Yoga*, 8 (1), 13–20.

Svaboda, Robert E. (2005). *Prakriti. Your Ayurvedic Constitution*. Motilal Benarsidass Publishers. Originally published 1999.

*The Agni Purana*. Natesa Gangadhara. Motilal Benarsidass.

*The Rig Veda*. (1986). (Wendy Doniger O'Flaherty, Trans.). Penguin Books.

Tiwari, Maya. (2002). *The Path of Practice. The Ayurvedic Book of Healing with Food, Breath and Sound*. Motilal Benarsidass.

Valiathan, M. S. (2003). *The Legacy of Caraka*. Orient Longman.

Wujastyk, D. (2001). *The Roots of Ayurveda: Selections from Sanskrit Medical Writings*. Penguin.

Wujastyk, G. and Smith F. M. (Eds.). (2008). *Modern and Global Ayurveda, Pluralism and Paradigms*. State University of New York Press.

## INTERNET RESOURCES

Ayurvedic Dosha Quiz: https://chopra.com/dosha-quiz#quiz

The Ayurvedic Institute: https://www.ayurveda.com/

Vaidyagram Ayurvedic Retreat Centre, Coimbatore, India: https://www.vaidyagrama.com/

Weintraub, A. (2024, January 5). *Yoga for Trauma*: https://www.amyweintraub.com/yoga-for-trauma/

# 6 Establishing Harmony: Health and Healing in Chinese Traditions

The various spiritual, religious, and philosophical traditions of China have developed over thousands of years. Confucianism, Daoism, Buddhism, and Chinese folk beliefs have all had an influence on the larger tradition. In turn, the vast cultural orbit of China has impacted the regions around it including Korea, Japan, and Vietnam.

Chinese thought does, however, have certain background assumptions. The most important central ideal being the belief in the need for establishing and maintaining harmony. As a result, there is an emphasis on harmonious political, social and familial relationships illustrated in the centrality of both ancestor worship and filial piety. From within this belief system the family is the primary unit of society.

From the perspective of Chinese Traditional Religion those who have died retain their status in the family and can influence the lives of their family members. The earliest records of Chinese history record practices of divination aimed at remaining in contact with ancestral spirits. Various systems of divination were used and have continued into the present with the *I-Ching* (Book of Changes) considered a sacred text.

Those overseeing communications with ancestors, and other shamanic functions, are among the first recorded religious specialists in Chinese culture. These figures, referred to as *wu*, were experts in exorcism, prophecy, fortune-telling, rain-making, and the interpretation of dreams. In their role in the Chinese royal courts and government they played a vital role in discerning the Will of Heaven. The Will of Heaven, in turn, was believed to have a direct impact on

DOI: 10.4324/9781003471769-6

political and social well-being of both the state and the communities within it.

Another foundational belief of Chinese traditions is in the Dao, the primordial energy from which all phenomenal reality emerges. This ground of being is seen as the source and basis of all life determining the laws of nature and human well-being. Emerging from the Dao are the principles of yin and yang which are the basis of constantly changing reality.

These two opposite, but complimentary energies, are seen as the building blocks of all phenomenal reality. Yin is associated with the feminine, coolness, wetness, and darkness, yang with brightness, heat, and openness. Each person is understood as embodying both elements although men are believed to be predominantly more yang and women more yin.

## TRADITIONAL CHINESE MEDICINE (TCM)

A concern with health and longevity has been a feature of Chinese thought from the earliest written records dating from 1766–1222 BCE. The sages of ancient China were particularly interested in finding the elixir of immortality and with living the longest, healthiest life possible.

The written history of Chinese medicine begins with the legend of the Yellow Emperor (Huangdi) who, according to myth, became the supreme ruler of the universe. Two medical works were attributed to the Yellow Emperor and the Fire Emperor called *The Yellow Emperor's Classic of Internal Medicine* (*Nei Jing*) and the *Classic of Herbal Medicine*.

This classic work has been likened to the works of Hippocrates in terms of its influence within Chinese medicine and is still a core text for those studying Traditional Chinese Medicine (TCM). The text includes philosophy, diagnostics, and instructions on the practice of acupuncture.

According to the *Nei Jing* in order to understand an illness one must understand the entire context, and observe the overall environment, emotions, and attitudes of the patients. The *Nei Jing* (2019) begins with the Yellow Emperor asking his physician why human beings no longer live to be a 100 years old. He is told that, "In the past people practiced Tao, the Way of Life. they understood the principles of the balance of yin and yang" (p. 1).

The Daoist tradition was a key influence on Chinese medicine with its focus on inner alchemy and the search for elixir of immortality. Practices of self-cultivation included working with herbs, breath, and forms of meditation. These practices emphasize the need for balance and harmony and guarding of energy.

Herbology is one of the pillars in the practice of TCM and extensive knowledge of healing plants is a central part of training. Many sacred narratives describe the origins of medicinal plants including gingko and angelica. From the point of view of TCM, the closer the preparation is to the original plant the better and growing fresh herbs remains central to practice.

In another narrative the character of Lady White, half-serpent, half-female, is described as running an apothecary shop known as the Temple of Preserved Harmony. The legends states that:

> When an epidemic broke out in Zhenjiang "those affected had yellowing complexions, atrophied muscles, and extremely low morale", she proclaimed that herbs were the answer, and then set out to gather them on the Mountain of a Hundred Plants. The afflicted population miraculously recovered after drinking her herbal remedies.
>
> *(Tan, 2003, p. 338)*

Many of the myths describe going to the sacred mountains to gather medicinal plants during times of epidemics.

During the Han era (206 BC–220 AD), the treatise known as the *Classic of Mountains and Seas* (*Shanhaijing*) covered fields of botany, zoology, and medicine. It contained numerous prescriptions for the use of medicinal botanicals to alleviate disease symptoms. The book recounts how ten shamans attempted to climb Mount Ling to discover "the hundred kinds of drugs", and how they used chants and herbs to cure diseases such as then prevalent malaria and scabies (Tan, 2003, p. 339).

More than 20,000 formulas have been described, but only about 2,000 are in current use. In Chinese herbal therapy, several herbs are compounded to treat multiple symptoms and causes, as well as to counteract any accompanying side effects. Chinese healing focuses on nutritional support for the various organs and purports to work through *chi* (energy) that reaches the organs through pathways known as meridians.

Prescriptions can be classified into four groups: the king herb, the minister or subject herb, the assistant herb, and the servant herb.

The king treats the cause or chief symptom and is aided by the minister that also neutralises any side effects from the king herb. The assistant herb provides backup reinforcement of the therapeutic effect, and further reduces side effects of both the king and minister drugs. Finally, the servant coordinates and leads the herbal remedy to the affected areas.

Current research has revealed that the mountain regions described in these narratives as sacred, in fact, act as plant refugia. Lopez-Pujol et al. (2011) note that the majority of China's plant diversity, "are located in just 10 areas, all of them in the southern mountain region"(p. 261). The biodiversity of this region has been demonstrated by how researchers have deemed the area refugia or "plant cradles".

## THE PHYSICIAN IN THE CHINESE TRADITION

The role of the physician emerges by the early centuries of the Common Era according to Chinese historical records. Doctors are described as performing surgery and practicing gynaecology, ophthalmology, and psychiatry and it is also likely that they practiced acupuncture.

The physician, Zhang Zhongjing, who lived at the end of the second century CE, has been referred to as the Chinese Hippocrates. Zhang is best known for his written work on typhoid and fever in which he called for the use of drugs and cooling baths. Zhang wrote on the symptoms and course of disease carefully recording the efficacy of various drugs.

Sun Simiao (*c*.581–682) born during the Tang Dynasty, was so revered that he has been referred to as the King of Medicine and apotheosized as the God of Medicine. His influential encyclopedia, *Essential Prescriptions*, discussed ethics and the role of the doctor drawing on Confucian, Daoist, and Buddhist ideas. Sun Simiao called on physicians to treat all people equally, to value life above all else, and to uphold the virtues of a sage/healer.

The writings of Sun Simiao emphasized *yang sheng* (nurturing life) to achieve health and longevity through self-cultivation. This included proper diet, paying attention to changing seasons and moderate exercise. *Yang Sheng* called for a regular and structured routine and moderation in all areas of life recognizing the intimate connection between mind and body.

The idea of only attending to health when one is sick is likened to a person who only starts to dig a well when he or she is thirsty or to forge weapons when the battle has already begun. "The superior physician" according to the Chinese maxim, "teaches the patient how to stay healthy".

## THE BODY IN CHINESE MEDICINE

Attitudes to the body in the Chinese tradition reveal the same complex mixture of Confucianism, Daoism, and Buddhism as the larger spiritual worldview. From the Confucian point of view the body is a gift from one's ancestors and must be treated with reverence. It is also the duty of the children as part of the practice of filial piety to ensure the longevity and well-being of their elders.

With the Buddhist tradition entering into China in the first decade of the Common Era it is very likely that the concept of the energies of the human body developed though syncretism. However, the world-affirming practical attitude of the Chinese has largely subsumed the more ascetic Buddhist view and we see a largely positive attitude towards the human body and life in the world.

This view of the body is based on an energetic and alchemical model. As part of this holistic understanding the mind and the body are not understood as separate units but as part of a system. From this perspective physical and mental symptoms are intimately related and cannot be separated from each other or the lifestyle of the person being examined.

From the perspective of Traditional Chinese Medicine (TCM), one of the primary ways that health is maintained is by supporting and preserving the various energies of the body. Human beings are understood as standing between heaven (*tien*) and earth (*di*) drawing power from both sources and so human health requires a proper harmony between these powers.

According to TCM *chi*/*qi* moves through meridians (*jing lou*) in the human body. Distortions or blockages in energy patterns are believed to be the basis of many diseases. From this point of view physical disease is the final manifestation of long-standing imbalances within the overall system. Diseases are cured by restoring and rebalancing the internal energies of the body and the goal is to detect abnormalities before they manifest as a serious disease.

The energies of the body are often referred to as the Three Treasures. The first of these is *jing* understood as being the essence or the life force that is inherited from one's parents. From the standpoint of TCM each individual needs to do their best to preserve and enhance their inheritance which includes proper diet, exercise and lifestyle. Factors such as stress, anxiety, and worry are also believed to deplete *jing*.

*Shen* is the most subtle of the three treasures and is believed to be what remains after the death of the physical body. This energy is also believed to be the seat of morality which guides human beings in proper actions. This allows the individual to think beyond themselves and about the good of the whole.

The third treasure is *chi/qi* and refers both to the totality of all the body's vital energies and to all the energy in the cosmos. *Qi/chi* is understood as being the most basic component of life and the energy that drives all manifestations of the phenomenal world that we see around us. It is understood as being the power behind the processes of nature and by extension those of the human body and mind. *Qi/chi* is the force that results in a leaf unfurling and in the beat of the human heart and so the human body is seen as being a microcosm of the larger system.

From the point of view of Chinese medical thought, it is typical to see the impact of unhealthy life choices in middle age as reserves of inherited energy begin to be depleted. Herbs, massage, and the practices of *tai chi* then are all meant to ensure that energy is consistently restored and maintained.

The quality of one's *qi/chi* is impacted by diet, by habitual emotions and by environment. Someone who is healthy then is not simply free of disease but has *qi/chi* that is flowing and is well nourished and supported by a healthy diet and environment and practices such as ritual and meditation.

Traditional Chinese Medicine is not as concerned about causality as allopathic medicine, but instead observes the whole system and looks for root patterns of disharmony. An example would be in treating infertility, the physician often looks at strengthening the kidney, spleen and liver and this is believed not only to allow for conception but to ensure that the woman has enough energy to carry the baby to term.

The TCM doctor assesses overall vitality by appearance and through questions and pulse diagnosis. Treatment will often consist of acupuncture, *Tui Na* (massage), cupping, breath work, and the prescription of herbs and lifestyle advice. The emphasis is placed on a holistic look at overall health and balancing the elements of yin and yang so they can function harmoniously.

## From the Nei Jing:

In the old days the sages treated disease by preventing illnesses before it began, just as a good government or emperor was able to take the necessary steps to avert war. Treating an illness after it has begun is like suppressing revolt after it has broken out. If someone digs a well when thirsty or forges weapons after becoming engaged in battle, one cannot help but ask: Are not these actions too late?

(Ni, 1995, p. 7)

## TRADITIONAL CHINESE MEDICINE IN THE CONTEMPORARY ERA

Traditional Chinese Medicine remains a foundational aspect of Chinese health care into the present. However, Traditional Chinese Medicine (TCM) has faced numerous challenges both in China and in the diaspora during the 20th century. With the coming to power of a Communist government in 1949 all religions came under suspicion.

The esteem in which the practices and doctors of TCM were held ensured its survival. Today in China TCM is a central part of mainstream health care with 2,000 hospitals and over 80,000 physicians offering its services (Chakrabarti, 2014, p. 196).

The Chinese state is also increasingly moving to support its practice through conferences and protection and restoration of historic sites related to TCM. The birthplace of medical sage Zhang Zhongjing, in Nanyang continues to be celebrated for its contribution to medicine. The government now supports regular public celebration of the contributions the medical sage Zhang Zhongjing. The area of Nanyang is traditionally viewed as a storehouse of natural remedies and remains so today with 2,356 species of TCM herbs being harvested there.

Increasingly, by the late 20th century, TCM has also made its way alongside diasporic communities in Australia, Canada, and the USA. Traditional Chinese Medicine and the practice of acupuncture has rapidly become one of the most popular forms of non-allopathic medicine. As more and more people began to consult practitioners of Chinese medicine, controversy was stirred regarding its legal status as a healing system in these countries.

In the Canadian case, where universal health care is delivered by the provinces, each has negotiated the position of TCM. The Ontario and British Columbia governments, both provinces with significant Chinese and Chinese-Canadian populations, acted upon calls for regulation. The year 2006 saw the proclamation of the Chinese Medicine Act and the creation of the The college of Traditional Chinese Medicine Practitioners and Acupuncturists of Ontario.

TCM has adapted within the Canadian system and taken on the organizational structures of the colleges of physicians and surgeons. This means that experts from within the field oversee their own practices operating within the overall rules of their jurisdiction. The College oversees the examination and credentialing of practitioners within the province in which it operates. This body also serves as a repository of information related to professional development, career opportunities and for filing complaints and finding a licensed practitioner.

In the United States the National Institutes of Health in the US act as a clearing house for information regarding different forms of healing such as TCM. Their website provides information on efficacy, safety, and licensing under the banner of the National Center for Complimentary and Integrative Health. Most states have laws regulating acupuncture practice and require certification by the National Certification Commission for Acupuncture and Oriental Medicine.

## *Xiaolan Zhao, Traditional Chinese Medical Doctor and MD.*

### A Vision for Healthcare Transformed

Walking in for an appointment at Xiaolan Health Centre one is instantly struck by the beauty of the space. The clinic resides in a renovated Victorian building nestled in the Annex neighbourhood of Toronto. Upon entering shoes are taken off and the main foyer is open, light and airy with plenty of natural light and art work. Sitting in the well-appointed waiting room with hardwood floors and art on the walls, is a statue of Kuan Yin the Goddess of Compassion.

The person behind this unusual healing space is Xiaolan Zhao. Zhao grew up in China during the Cultural Revolution and by 1986 was working as a general surgeon in an emergency department in Kunming, China. Unable to stop the bleeding of a 24-year-old woman Zhao called upon her knowledge of traditional herbal medicine. The success of this treatment led her on the path to studying Traditional Chinese Medicine (TCM). Within her practice Zhao brings together TCM and other healing modalities under one roof.

Zhao (2012) recognizes her connection with the ancient healing tradition of China and writes, "I am descended from a great tradition of learning about the human body, mind and soul that is thousands of years old and informed by the wisdom of Taoist philosophers. They saw each body as a microcosm of the universe. When we live according to the laws of nature, we live in harmony and health" (p. 27).

Zhao has observed that in China the majority of patients had a yang deficiency whereas in Canada many patients are lacking in yin energy. She argues this is a reflection of the overriding emphasis on busyness and achievement in North American society. Activity, movement, speed, growth, expansion, youth, and patriarchy epitomize our culture. Zhao advises, "to balance the Yang quality of western culture I suggest Yin activity such as inward moments of stillness. Walking among trees, sitting quietly or meditation" (p. 27).

From the Xiaolan Health Centre website.

I believe that by integrating Eastern and Western medical traditions we can provide the best possible health care for patients. Currently, most doctors practice reactive medicine. Once they have an immediate problem under control, they devote virtually no time to patients' ongoing health. True health care, by contrast, shows how to prevent disease from recurring. Its practitioners address the whole body, teaching patients to change their lifestyles in ways that encourage better health while discouraging illness.

The goal of Xiaolan Health Centre is to be a model for this superior approach to health care. We bring together the best of the world's great medical traditions, taking the time required to assess, diagnose, and develop an individual plan of treatment for each patient. At the same time, we educate people on what caused their health issues in the first place and give them the tools they need to achieve and sustain wellness throughout their lives.

## OVERVIEW OF CHINESE TRADITIONS

Estimated Number of Followers:

Confucians: 6–20 million

Daoists: 30 million

Chinese Popular Religion: 100–300 million

Found in East Asia and in large diasporas in South East Asia, Singapore, and North America.

Important Beliefs and Practice: maintenance of harmony, filial piety, ancestor worship.

Texts:

Confucianism: the Five Classics and Four Books.

Daoists: Daodejing and Zhuangzi part of large of canon of over 1,000 books.

Important Leaders:

For Confucians: Confucius, Mencius, and Xunzi.

For Daoists: Laozi and Zhuangzi.

The Chinese have practiced both burial and cremation with the government encouraging cremation after the Communist Revolution of 1949. Families may maintain an ancestral shrine or practice grave visitation.

## REFERENCES

Chakrabarti, Pratik. (2014). *Medicine and Empire, 1600–1960*. Palgrave Macmillan.

Tan, S. Y. (2003). Medicine in Stamps. Li Shih-Chen (1518–1593) Herbalist of Renown. *Singapore Medical Journal*, 44(7), 338–9.

*The Yellow Emperor's Classic of Medicine: A New Translation of the Nei Jing*. (2019). Maoshing Ni (Trans.). Shambhala.

Zhao, Xiaolan. (2012). *Inner Beauty Through Traditional Chinese Medicine*. Vintage Canada.

Zhao, Xiaolan. (2006). *Reflections of the Moon on Water: Healing Women's Bodies and Minds Through Traditional Chinese Wisdom*. Vintage Canada.

## FURTHER READING

Deng, Tietao and Kevin Ergil. (1999). *Practical Diagnosis in Traditional Chinese Medicine*. Churchill Livingstone.

Eight Traditional Chinese Herbs Laid at Zhang Zhongjing Temple, China Daily (1994), updated October 31, 2019. *Chinese Medicine*. Random House.

*Immortal Sisters. Secret Teachings of Taoist Women*. (1999). Thomas Cleary (Trans). North Atlantic Books. Originally published 1989.

Lao Tzu. (1963). *Tao Te Ching*. D. C. Lau (Trans). Penguin Books.

Li, Zhaoguo, Wu Qing, and Xing Yurui. (2019). *Key Concepts in Traditional Chinese Medicine*. Palgrave Pivot.

Lihong, Liu. (2019). *Classical Chinese Medicine*. Gabriel Weiss and Henry Buchtel (Trans.). Chinese University Press.

Lu, Yubin and Chengcai Liu. (1997). *Concepts and Theories of Traditional Chinese Medicine*. Science Press.

Men, Jiuzhang, and Lei Guo. (2010). *A General Introduction to Traditional Chinese Medicine*. Science Press/CRC Press.

Reid, Daniel. (1996). *The Shambhala Guide to Traditional Chinese Medicine*. Shambhala.

Ryan, Mary Kay. (2011). Infusing Chinese Medicine with Spirit. Daosim, Shamanism and Chinese Medicine in the Modern World. *Journal of Daoist Studies*, 4, 175–89.

*Traditional Chinese Medicine: Professionalization and Integration in Hong Kong*. Kara Chan and Dong Dong (Eds.). City University of Hong Kong.

Unschuld, Paul U. (2018). *Traditional Chinese Medicine: Heritage and Adaptation*. Columbia University Press.

Wang, Chen-Kuo, P'ing Hsieh, and Peiping Xie. (1999). *History and Development of Traditional Chinese Medicine*. Science Press.

Wilms, Sabine. (June 2010). Nurturing Life in Classical Chinese Medicine: Sun Simiao on Healing Without Drugs, Transforming Bodies and Cultivating Life. *The Journal of Chinese Medicine*.

Yuan, Chun-Su, Eric J. Bieber, and A. Brent. (2011). *Concepts and Theories of Traditional Chinese Medicine*. CRC Press.

Zhang, Zhongjing. (1986). *Treatise on Febrile Diseases Caused by Cold. Shangun Lun*. New World Press.

## INTERNET RESOURCES

College of Traditional Chinese Medicine Practitioners and Acupuncturists of British Columbia: https://www.ctcmpao.on.ca

College of Traditional Chinese Medicine Practitioners and Acupuncturists of Ontario: https://www.ctcmpao.on.ca

National Institutes of Health, Traditional Chinese Medicine: What You Need to Know: https://www.nccih.nih.gov/health/traditional-chinese-medicine-what-you-need-to-know

# 7 May All Be Free From Suffering: Buddhism and Healing

Buddhism was founded in the 6th century BCE in the area straddling the border of what is now India and Nepal by Siddhhartha Gautama and is now an international religion practiced all around the globe. The Buddhist tradition emerged from the powerful insights of its founder around the causes of human suffering how it can be remedied.

Over the millennia Buddhism has evolved into three enduring streams of Theravada, Mahayana, and Vajrayana. While these three display many differences, they share an emphasis on wisdom and compassion. All three developed monastic institutions for both monks and nuns which have been important sites of teaching and repositories of knowledge.

Buddhists developed a sophisticated spiritually-based psychology regarding the importance of the mind as an avenue for achieving enlightenment and liberation. The *Dhammapada* states in the oldest strata of the scripture if a person speaks or acts, "from a impure mind suffering follows him as the wheel of the cart follows the beast that draws the cart" (Dhammapada 1.1).

Theravada Buddhism was carried out of the Indian subcontinent through Sri Lanka and into Southeast Asia (Thailand, Laos, Cambodia) Mahayana Buddhism travelled along the Silk Road and into China beginning in 0 CE. From there Buddhist teachings spread to Korea, Vietnam, and Japan. Vajrayana Buddhism was taken by charismatic teachers to the Tibetan and Himalayan region where it mixed with the Indigenous traditions.

Everywhere it has travelled for over 2,500 years Buddhism has been directly connected to healing. The Buddhist view of health and

DOI: 10.4324/9781003471769-7

healing emerges from its central concern with suffering and compassion. From the beginning the Buddha was described as the Great Physician who diagnosed the disorders that cause suffering to all humanity. Through the Four Noble Truths he laid out the problem and offered the cure with the Noble Eightfold Path.

Because Buddhism spread throughout Asia, Buddhist concepts have influenced Tibetan, Central, and East Asian approaches to medicine.

Kenneth Zysk (2010) noting Buddhism's role in the codifying, teaching, and the practice of medicine writes that "In India, and elsewhere in Asia, Buddhism throughout its history maintained a close relationship with the healing arts" (6).

From the Buddhist perspective the only true healing for anyone, regardless of the affliction, is a radical change in consciousness and movement towards enlightenment. From this point of view all human beings live on a continuum of various types of suffering that require healing. Some form of suffering is endemic to the human condition and can only be cured by following the teachings of the tradition.

Buddhism also recognizes that the human body is always vulnerable to disease and that all are in the process of aging. In the story of the Four Sights, it is the sight of a sick person that contributes to Siddhartha Gautama's decision to renounce the world and become the Buddha (the awakened one).

The *Mahavagga*, depicts the first known instance of healing in the tradition. In this earliest section of the scripture there is the description of the Buddha visiting a group of monks and finding that one is seriously ill. Seeing that none was caring for him the Buddha attended the monk himself. Afterwards he propounded the rule binding on the monks stating:

> You, O bhikkus, have neither a mother or a father who could nurse you. If, O bhikkus, you do not nurse one another, who then will nurse you? Whoever, O bhikkus would nurse me, he should nurse the sick.
>
> *(MV 8.26.3)*

This incident in the most sacred part of the Buddhist canon establishes the link between Buddhist ethics and health care from the beginning.

In the Pali canon of Buddhism, the various causes of illness are listed. These include karma alongside more empirical causes such as change of season and its influence on the humours or *doshas* of the body—concepts shared with the Ayurvedic tradition. However, karmic reasons for sickness are downplayed in comparison to strictly physical causes. The fact that the Buddha himself was described as falling ill on various occasions demonstrates the purely physical nature of many disorders.

Monks and nuns acted as healers and collected a vast store house of medical knowledge across the Buddhist world. The first documented codification of this medical lore took place as wandering ascetics assumed a more stationary existence in the early Buddhist monasteries. Over time Buddhist monasteries became centres of knowledge with large libraries and developed into universities such as Nalanda in North western India.

Medical manuals were passed down alongside scripture describing various conditions and how they were to be treated. These records included a growing pharmacopoeia which featured a wide variety of roots, fats, gums, resin, salts, herbal prescriptions, and extracts. Medicine was also deemed one of the only acceptable possessions for a nun or monk alongside their begging bowl and robe.

The attitude of the Buddha towards the medical profession was a straightforward one and he is described as consulting physicians in the Pali canon. It was expected that a person who became ill would seek out medical advice while also engaging in acts of penance and charity in an effort to mitigate the results of the karma. Suffering in this sense, then, has both a physical and moral component.

The most important doctor mentioned in the early literature was Jivaka Kumabhrta who was referred to as the "King of Physicians" (Salguero, 2022, p. 22). Jivaka is described as performing surgeries and giving medications. Over time he has taken on the role of the ideal physician and continues to be honoured in countries like Thailand and China.

Buddhism also developed princples regarding public welfare. The Emperor Ashoka, who reigned *c.*265–238 BCE in what is now northern India, is often considered the template of Buddhist social welfare ideals. Ashoka was considered a Chakravartin whose political power was put in the service of the Buddhist dharma. His rock edicts, which have survived into the present, stated that medical treatments, both for human beings and animals, were to be made available and medicinal plants cultivated.

The Buddhist tradition was a vital driver of the creation of hospitals and dispensaries across South and East Asia. In Buddhist influenced societies governments could make merit and be seen as benevolent by undertaking these projects.

## ATTITUDES TOWARDS THE BODY IN BUDDHISM

The early Buddhist traditions demonstrated a distinct distrust of the senses that were seen as ensnaring the individual in karmic bonds. This is part of the larger logic of asceticism and as a result attitudes towards the body, at least in the early tradition, tend be one of suspicion. Descriptions of the human body emphasize its impermanence and the danger of anchoring one's identity in it.

The body, in Theravada Buddhism, is understood as being in a state of constant flux and decay. From this point of view, it doesn't make sense to look for any state of permanence within the body or the mind. Attachment to the body, then, is viewed as a source of bondage and we see in the story of the Four Sights the young prince Siddhartha Gautama is shocked to think that his body too is subject to illness, old age, and death.

However, Buddhism was also referred to as the Middle Way situated between the severe forms of asceticism practiced by traditions such as Jainism and life of hedonistic self-indulgence. The Buddha was very clear that one should never intentionally harm the body and this was viewed by Buddhists and breaking the law of *ahimsa* or non-harmfulness. Buddhism forbids deliberately harming one's own body or that of another person.

Buddhists took a pragmatic approach that a healthy body as it was needed to seek liberation. Being born as a human being was seen as great good fortune as it was only from this state that nirvana could be attained. The body of oneself and others, then, was to be treated with care but not indulged.

## BUDDHIST UNDERSTANDING OF KARMA AND HEALTH

The belief in karma, the law of cause and effect over multiple life times, also influences Buddhist ideas about health and healing. From the perspective of the tradition it is only from this position that *nirvana* (enlightenment) can be achieved.

As a result, each individual is encouraged to live as consciously as possible. The body and personality are understood as being conditioned by past lives, and choices made within those lives. However, within this present life time it is up to the individual to choose actions based on moral precepts that will lead eventually towards liberation. As Harvey (1990) puts it, "the law of karma is not viewed as rigid and mechanical but as the flexible, fluid, dynamic outworking of the fruits of action" (p. 42).

Buddhists generally recognize that karma impacts upon health. The body that we are born into, with its strengths and weaknesses, is understood as being a direct result of past karma. Also, this interpretation presupposes that there is a direct link between morality and health. Health depends on our choices regarding lifestyle and illness from this perspective is linked to unhealthy choices in all areas of life.

Also if the disease is a result of karma, from this point of view, it cannot be cured until the moral context is addressed and the negative karma is burned off. These can include a variety of actions including acts of giving selfless service, fasting, pilgrimage and development of wisdom through meditation practices, chanting of scripture, and prayer.

From the Buddhist point of view the individual also has to take responsibility for maintaining good health through their own efforts. These include proper diet and eschewing unhealthy substances such as intoxicants. Buddhists are usually taught to avoid drugs and alcohol in the fifth precept. One should not abuse the body with food, alcohol, or drugs or through either overindulgence or deprivation. However, as it is recognized that the causes of illness are complex from a Buddhist point of view compassion is always the correct response.

As Ratanakul (1999) writes, once it has been determined that death is inevitable then the caregiver must turn their attention to "compassionate care of the dying, their main concern being to relieve the suffering of patients and families and ensure a good death" (p. 26). Buddhist cultures around the world have developed various rituals to ease the passage, emphasize consciousness and contribute to a positive rebirth and have been involved in hospice care.

## HEALTH AND HEALING IN MAHAYANA BUDDHISM

The Mahayana stream of Buddhism branched off from Theravada beginning in the 4th century BCE. This took root in East Asia along the Silk Road spreading from China to Korea and Japan. Mahayana Buddhism developed its own philosophies, world views and ritual practices however it retained and emphasized the Buddhist virtue of compassion.

The Mahayana tradition builds on the Buddhist insight that all human beings are subject to the "poisons of the mind" such as anger, greed and envy. These, in turn had to be transformed through practices that emphasized the qualities of loving kindness (*metta*), sympathetic joy and rejoicing in the good fortune of others (*mudita*), and eqanimity (*upekkha*).

Whereas the Theravadin Buddhists viewed the Buddha as an exemplary man who achieved enlightenment and could serve as a revered exemplar, in the Mahayana tradition the Buddha was viewed as a deity. Alongside the historical Buddha a growing pantheon of supernatural beings developed. The centrality of the virtue of compassion was developed fully within the figure of the bodhisattva. The bodhisattva was an enlightened being who had foregone nirvana in order to help those who were still suffering.

While the bodhisattvas were understood as being divine, all Buddhists were encouraged to imitate their selflessness and self-sacrifice by taking bodhisattva vows. With these vows, one makes the promise to work for the complete enlightenment of all sentient beings. Shantideva writes in the *The Way of the Bodhisattva* (2006):

> May every being ailing with disease
>
> Be freed at once from every malady.
>
> May every sickness that afflicts the living
>
> Be wholly and forever absent from the world.
>
> May those who go in dread have no more fear
>
> May captives be unchained and now set free.
>
> And may the weak receive their strength.
>
> May living beings help each other in kindness.
>
> *(p. 166)*

Desiring the well-being of others is seen as benefiting both the world and one's self. From a Mahayana perspective the practice of healing is a primary expression of compassion and part of the larger bodhisattva path.

One of the bodhisattvas most connected with health and well-being is Kwan Yin (She Who Hears the Prayers of the World). Known as the Goddess of mercy, Kwan Yin is petitioned as a great healer who can cure all ills. Kwan Yin is associated particularly with the concerns of women and women's health and is often depicted holding a child.

It is believed that calling her name in time of crisis may grant deliverance. Statues of Kwan Yin can be found in public forms in East Asia and are also used in practices of home worship.

Another bodhisattva associated with health and healing is the Medicine Buddha or Bhaisajyaguru. This bodhisattva is worshipped across the Mahayana Buddhist world and is described as being azure blue, holding a bowl filled with healing nectar and holding a bowl filled with healing nectar and the "great medicine", the myrobalan plant (*a-ru-ra*). The Seventh Great Vow of the Medicine Buddha states:

> Sentient beings afflicted with various illnesses, with no one to help them, nowhere to turn, no physicians, no medicine, no family, no home, - who are destitute and miserable-will, as soon as my name passes their ears, be relieved of all their illnesses.
>
> *(Thanh, 2001, p. 21)*

The Medicine Buddha is believed to protect living beings from physical and mental sickness as well as other dangers and obstacles.

The bodhisattva is also believed to help to eradicate the three poisons—attachment, hatred, and ignorance. Sacred narratives describe the Medicine Buddha as emanating from the heart of the Buddha and gave instructions on how to recite the mantra for oneself and for others, for sick and dying people and how to perform many different healing rituals.

## Thamkrabok Monastery and Rehabilitation Centre

Thamkrabok Monastery was founded in 1957 by two brothers based on the teachings of their aunt, a holy woman renowned for her healing abilities. After Thailand implemented strict anti-drug legislation in the 1950s the monks of Thamkrabok Wat (monastery) began to work with those who were addicted to drugs. Some of its earliest patients were men who had become addicted to heroin during the

Vietnam war. This established the pattern of the monastery taking in those struggling with addiction regardless of nationality or religious background.

The approach practiced within the monastery emphasizes personal responsibility. According to Abbot Luang Poh Charoen healing has only 5% to do with body. From a Buddhist perspective addiction to a substance is simply one extreme form of craving that is the cause of all human suffering. The larger goal which is to purify the poisons of the mind will, in turn, move the person away from addictive patterns. The Buddhist injunction against intoxicants is related to this ultimate goal of a clear and calm consciousness.

Those who undergo rehabilitation at Thamkrabok are only permitted to go through the process once and are expected to go “cold turkey”. The *sajja* (vow) is referred to on the official Thamkrabok website as the most important part of the treatment. If the patient is Buddhist this will have a powerful impact but even if the vow taker is not Buddhist the religious setting gives weight to the promise. The patient takes the vow:

> I will not smoke consume or inject, I will not encourage others to smoke, consume, or inject, I will not possess or encourage others to possess, I will not buy or sell any kind of addictive drugs including opiates, cocaine, cannabis, gatom leaves, or methamphetamines for the rest of my life.

Visitors are expected to keep the same rigorous schedule as the monks getting up early and performing a variety of chores such as sweeping and gardening.

A variety of techniques are used at the monastery including a physical detoxification that includes the use of herbal steam baths and black pills that are taken daily. While at Thamkrabok those who are going through rehabilitation can participate in 12-step groups and have access to counseling by senior monks. Meditation classes are offered every morning as well as dhamma (dharma) talks, and chanting in the evening.

Upon completion of the programme the abbot gives a ring to the successful person who completes the programme. These rituals are concrete markers of the achievement and also a physical reminder for the person wearing the ring of their vow to remain sober. In some cases, patients become ordained as monks and stay on at the monastery to help others.

Thamkrabok has attracted worldwide attention for its success and affordability. Whereas rehabilitation centres in places like the US can cost up to $30,000 a month—Thamkrabok offers its services free of charge. The National Healthcare System in the UK has also recognized the efficacy and affordability of the practice and has sent patients to Thailand. A wide variety of Buddhist based approaches specifically aimed at treating addiction have now been developed around the Buddhist world.

## MINDFULNESS AND THE CONTEMPORARY CONNECTION BETWEEN BUDDHISM AND PSYCHOLOGY

Buddhism has increasingly influenced western society as a result of the 1960s counterculture and a growing Buddhist diaspora in the western world. Books written on the topic of Buddhism by writers such a Thich Nhat Hanh and Pema Chodron have consistently reached a wide audience. Both of these traditional renunciants have brought ancient teachings to the public in ways that speak to our cultural moment.

Buddhist approaches to the mind have continued to influence western forms of psychology. Vipassana meditation is considered to be the oldest of the Buddhist meditative techniques and the person mediating observes as events and emotions rise and fall without attaching to them in any way. Another type of meditation found in the Pali canon is *Samatha* or serenity meditation aimed at entering into states of consciousness that eventually lead to the cessation of suffering.

One of the most influential pioneers in bringing meditation practices in to the mainstream is American medical doctor Jon Kabat-Zinn. Kabatt-Zinn graduated as a molecular biologist and also trained in traditional forms of Buddhist meditation. He has introduced many Buddhist practices into the western world shorn of overt religious context.

Kabat-Zinn founded the Stress Reduction Clinic and Center for Mindfulnes in Medicine, Healthcare and Society at the University of Massachusetts in 1995. In his best seller *Full Catastrophe Living* (2013) Kabat-Zinn discusses Mindfulness Stress Based Reduction (MSBR) introducing Buddhist concepts such as Beginners Mind and Non-Striving to mainstream, western audience. While making these ideas available to the public Kabat-Zinn (2013) is clear that they derive from Buddhism writing that, "it is no accident that mindfulness comes out of Buddhism, which has as its overriding concerns the relief of suffering and the dispelling of illusion" (lxii).

The eight-week Mindfulness Based Stress Reduction (MBSR) curriculum pioneered at University of Massachusetts is now being offered around the world. Consisting of training in awareness and meditative techniques that include body scans and non-judgmental awareness. First used in tandem with medical treatments at hospitals, these courses are now being taught in a wide variety of settings. Since then, training in mindfulness has expanded exponentially with centres for training springing up in many of the larger cities across North America.

Kabat-Zinn (2013) makes clear that the techniques being taught are not merely aimed at relaxation. They are a doorway into a completely different way of understanding health and well-being. He advocates for a change from the body as machine worldview and for the idea of "participatory medicine". Kabat-Zinn argues that while pain is a universal human phenomenon how we react, the phenomenon of suffering, is culturally mediated. Study after study has demonstrated that those trained in mindfulness find themselves better able to both re-frame and live with chronic pain (p. 370).

Increasingly mindfulness practices are being used as part of the tool kit of psychologists and counselors and have been found to be as effective as pharmaceuticals in treating condition likes anxiety and depression. The practice of different forms of meditation and mindfulness have become so mainstream they are now being covered by the National Health Service of the UK.

Buddhist retreats, meanwhile, have never been more popular and the weary and stressed citizens of North America vote with their feet. In Thailand, Myanmar, Tibet, Taiwan Buddhist medicine is fully integrated with larger healthcare systems. The tradition's insights regarding the human condition and techniques for working with emotions and the mind have never seemed more relevant.

## *Loving Kindness Meditation—Metta Bhavana*

May all beings:
… be free from anger.
… be free from ill will.

... be free from jealousy.
... be free from mental suffering.
... be free from physical suffering.
May all beings live in peace.
May all beings live happily.

Excerpted from Buddhist Meditation Centre of Halton

## REFLECTIONS

1. Why do you think meditative and mindfulness practices are so popular?
2. Do you think meditation practices have a place in our health-care system?
3. Why do you think the ideal of compassion appears again and again in Buddhist approaches to healing?

## OVERVIEW OF BUDDHISM

Founded by the Buddha, born Siddhartha Gautama in the kingdom of what is now Nepal, *c*.531 BCE.

Estimated number of followers: between 200 and 300 million with the majority in South East and East Asian but with significant populations all over the globe.

Major Branches: Theravada (Sri Lanka, South East Asia), Mahayana (East Asia), and Vajrayana (Tibet, Nepal).

Central Points of Philosophy:

The Four Noble Truths

1. The Noble Truth of Suffering (*dukkha*): This is the teaching that no human being can escape suffering whether it be physical or psychological.
2. The Noble Truth of the Origin of Suffering: Suffering arises from craving/desire (*trishna*).
3. The Noble Truth of Cessation: Suffering will cease when desire ceases.
4. The Noble Truth of the Eightfold Path: Suffering can be ended by ending craving by following the Eightfold Path.

The Noble Eightfold Path:

1. right understanding (based in Buddhist teachings)
2. right thought (free of desire, ill will cruelty)
3. right speech
4. right conduct
5. right livelihood (one's livelihood should not cause harm to other sentient beings)
6. right effort
7. right mindfulness
8. right meditation

Five Precepts: 1. to abstain from taking life; 2. to abstain from taking what is not given; 3. to abstain from sensuous misconduct; 4. to abstain from false speech; 5. to abstain from intoxicants as tending to cloud the mind. Monks and nuns follow three extra precepts that emphasize detachment from worldly life.

Three Jewels: The Buddha, The Dharma (teachings), and the Sangha (community).

Beliefs Regarding the Afterlife:

Buddhism teaches that there are various earthly, heaven, and hell realms through which consciousness transmigrates based on karma. While Mahayana traditions emphasize heaven realms as the goal Theravada teaches that the only way out of the cycle of samsara the continual process of birth, death, and rebirth is through the achievement of nirvana.

Buddhists generally practice cremation and emphasize the state of consciousness of the person while dying as this is believed to impact the next lifetime.

## REFERENCES

May all be freed from Suffering, from the Four Immeasuarables: https://www.westchesterbuddhistcenter.org/the-practice-of-the-four-immeasurablesHarvey, Peter. (2013). *An Introduction to Buddhism. Teachings, History and Practices. Second Edition*. Cambridge University Press. Originally published 1990.

Kabatt-Zinn, Jon. (2013). *Full Catastrophe Living. Using the Wisdom of Your Body and Mind to Face Stress, Pain and Illness*. Bantam Books. Originally published 1990.

Ratanakul, Pinit. (1999). Buddhist Healthcare Ethics. *Cross-Cultural Dialogue on Healthcare Ethics*. Wilfrid Laurier University Press.

Salguero, C. Pierce. (2022). *A Global History of Buddhism and Medicine*. Columbia University Press.

Shantideva. (2006). *The Way of the Bodhisattva*. Translated by Bodhicahrya-vatara and revised by the Padmakara Translation Group. Shambhala.

Thanh, Minh. (trans) (2001). *Sutra of the Medicine Buddha*. International Buddhist Monastic Institute.

Zysk, Kenneth G. (2010). *Asceticism and Healing in Ancient India. Medicine in The Buddhist Monastery*. Motilal Benarsidass. Originally published in 1991.

## FURTHER READING

Anālayo. (2015). Healing in Early Buddhism. *Buddhist Studies Review*, 32 (1), 19–33.

Birnbaum, Raoul. (1989). Chinese Buddhist Tradition of Healing and the Life Cycle. *Healing and Restoring: Health and Medicine in the World's Religious Traditions*. Lawrence E. Sullivan (Ed.). Macmillan Publishing Company.

Birnbaum, Raoul. (1989). *The Healing Buddha*. Shambhala.

*Buddhism and Medicine: An Anthology of Modern and Contemporary Sources*. (2020). C. Pierce Salguero (Ed.). Columbia University Press.

*Buddhist Healing in Medieval China and Japan*. (2020). C. Pierce Salguero and Andrew Macomber (Eds.). University of Hawaii Press.

Deane, Susannah. (2018). *Tibetan Medicine, Buddhism and Psychiatry: Mental Health and Healing in a Tibetan Exile Community*. Academic Press.

Dzogchen Ponlop Rinpoche. May All Be Well. The Aspirations of the Medicine Buddha. *Lion's Roar*, December 17, 2021.

Kilty, Gavin. (2010). *A Mirror of Beryl. A Historical Introduction to Tibetan Medicine*. Wisdom.

Kitagawa, Joseph Misuo. (1989). Buddhist Medical History. *Healing and Restoring. Health and Medicine in the World's Religious Traditions*. Lawrence E. Sullivan (Ed.). Macmillan Publishing Company.

Köhle, Natalie. (2021). Buddhism and Healing in China. *Encyclopedia of Religion*. Oxford University Press.

Liyanaratne, Jinadasa. (1999). *Buddhism and Traditional Medicine in Sri Lanka*. Kelaniya University Press.

Lo, Vivienne and Christopher Cullen (Eds.) (2005). *Medieval Chinese Medicine. The Duanhuang Medical Manuscripts*. Routledge Curzon.

Naqvi, Nasim H. (2011). *A Study of Buddhist Medicine and Surgery in Gandhara*. Motilal Benarsidass.

Patton, Thomas Nathan. (2018). *The Buddha's Wizards. Magic, Protection and Healing in Burmese Buddhism*. Columbia University Press.

Salguero, C. Pierce. (2017). *Buddhism and Medicine: An Anthology of Pre-modern Sources*. Columbia University Press.

Strickmann, Michel. (2002). *Chinese Magical Medicine*. Bernard Faure (Ed.). Stanford University Press.

*The Knowledge of Healing*. (2004). Dir. Franz Reichle, Icarus Films. 89 minutes.

Thich Nhat Hanh. (2006). *Transformation and Healing. Sutra on the Four Establishments of Mindfulness*. Parallax Press.

*The Dhammapada. The Path of Perfection*. (1982). Translated by Juan Mascaro. Penguin Books. Originally published 1973.

*Tibetan Medicine. A Buddhist Approach to Healing*. (2015). Dir. Sheldon Rochlin and Mikki Maher, 29 minutes.

Treleaven, David A. (2018). *Trauma-Sensitive Mindfulness. Practices for Safe and Transformative Healing*. W.W. Norton.

Triplett, Katja. (2019). *Buddhism and Medicine in Japan: A Topical Survey (500–1600 CE) of a Complex Relationship*. De Gruyter.

Yoeli-Tlalim, Ronit. (2021). *ReOrienting Histories of Medicine: Encounters Along the Silk Road*. Bloomsbury.

## INTERNET RESOURCES

Blue Beryl, Buddhism, Asian Medicine, Embodied Spirituality: http://www.piercesalguero.com/bio/

Buddhist Alcohol and Drug Rehab Centers, AddicitionResource.net: https://www.addictionresource.net/treatment/religious/buddhist/

Buddhist Healthcare in Philadelphia. (2018). Director, Cinematographer. The Jivaka Project: Buddhist Health and Healing. http://www.jivaka.net/philly-mainstream-healthcare

Healing Community Trauma at Seabrook Temple. (2018). Director, Cinematographer. The Jivaka Project: Buddhist Health and Healing. https://www.jivaka.net/philly-social-dimensions

Healing Buddha Mantra: https://www.youtube.com/watch?v=YUC9pU28g-k

Stress Reduction Clinic and Center for Mindfulness: https://dayofdifference.org.au/u-medical/university-of-massachusetts-medical-center-stress-reduction-clinic.html

Sutra of the Medicine Buddha: http://www.buddhanet.net/pdf_file/medbudsutra.pdf

Thailand's Rehab Temple. *Assignment Asia*, May 16, 2016, https://www.youtube.com/watch?v=Ozv4oRZHtkY

Wat Thamkrabok Official Website: https://wat-thamkrabok.org/

# 8 I am the Lord Your Healer: Health and Healing in the Jewish Tradition

The Jewish tradition emerged in the area now called Israel and Palestine and has been shaped by political events throughout its long history. Beginning with the patriarch Abraham the tradition consolidated into a community bound by laws, commandments, and ethics. Currently the majority of Jewish people live in Israel and in countries such as Russia, the United States, Canada, France, and England.

Jews have traditionally understood themselves to be in a covenant with God that requires certain obligations revealed to the community through the first patriarch Abraham, Noah, and the central prophet Moses. The words of later prophets believed to be the mouthpieces of the divine are recorded in the scriptures. While many Jews are religiously observant the tradition also recognizes itself as a culture regardless of religious belief or lack thereof.

Judaism is a monotheistic religion that understands the working out of the will of God in history. It has been said that the Jewish tradition is founded on Israel, the Torah, and prophets. Jews have traditionally emphasized the importance of moral action within the world and care for others.

Because the Jewish tradition developed in an area shaped by multiple empires this has had a decisive influence on the religion. A defining event was the destruction of the Temple in Jerusalem in 70 CE by the Romans. With their most holy site destroyed most of the Jewish population entered into a diaspora (*galut*) and existed as a minority tradition within either Muslim or Christian societies.

DOI: 10.4324/9781003471769-8

The restructuring and adaptation of the religion resulted in rabbinic Judaism which emerged with the figure of the rabbi and the institution of the synagogue becoming central. Over time different streams of Judaism developed including the Hasidic, Orthodox, Conservative, and Reform. The mystical beliefs and practices of Kabbalah that flourished in medieval Eastern Europe continue into the present.

Because of their status as a minority the Jewish tradition has been shaped by the idea of exile and ongoing anti-Semitism. In European history this has included expulsions from countries like Spain, Portugal, and England and limits on occupation, property ownership, and access to education.

The culmination of centuries of anti-Semitism in the Holocaust, in which at least six million Jews lost their lives, was a watershed in the history of the tradition. This resulted in growing calls for a nation state which came in to being as Israel in 1948.

Jewish attitudes towards healing have been shaped over time by many different forces one of the most important being the impact of the diaspora. In the case of the Ashkenazi Jewish communities that settled in Europe, they were often forced to live separated from the rest of European society and as a result developed their own systems which were in essence miniature welfare states with institutions of learning and healing.

The impact of being a minority tradition continued in the North American setting as Jews faced quota systems in universities and medical schools and, as a result, often founded their own hospitals. The issue of the safety and security of the Jewish community has remained central after the catastrophic impacts of the Holocaust.

The connection between religion and healing can be traced back to the beginnings of the Jewish tradition. In the Hebrew Bible staying in close connection with God through practices such as sacrifice, prayer, and repentance were all understood as maintaining a healthy life. Exodus 15:26 states, "for I am the Lord your healer" and the divine is understood as being the true source of well-being either directly or through a physician or other healer.

In the second book of Kings the actions of the prophet Elisha as a healer are described:

> When Elisha came into the house, he saw the child lying dead on his bed. He went in and shut the door upon the two of them and prayed to the Lord. Then he went up and lay upon the child, putting his mouth upon his mouth, his eyes upon his

> eyes, and his hands upon his hands and as he stretched himself upon him the flesh of the child became warm. The mother was called in and "she fell at his feet bowing to the ground".
>
> *(2 Kings 4:32–35)*

The prophets Elisha and Elijah are both depicted as being able to perform miraculous forms of healing. This power was directly linked to their intimate connection with the divine.

The Jewish emphasis on the sacredness of life is central to all forms of heath and healing. This is expressed in the well-known Jewish dictum that one who "saves the life of a single person, Scripture imputes to him as though he had saved the whole world". The tradition also emphasizes the integrity and dignity of life (*kavod*) regardless of the physical challenges being faced. The body was seen as created by God and therefore to be honoured and respected.

The practice of visiting the sick (*bikkur cholim*) is mandated by the Jewish tradition. Drawing on Biblical models such as the Book of Job this practice is considered to be obligatory. Springer (2013) emphasizes the importance of, "presence, attunement and drawing near" (p. 83). Being fully present and listening is considered to be better than any attempts at resolving or problem solving.

The Talmud, the scripture based on Jewish oral tradition, contains a variety of approaches to health which include attention to diet, rest, massage, and herbs. The texts also recognize the importance of clean air and sun light which were seen as being vital to maintaining and restoring health. These sources reveal knowledge of a variety of diseases and the practice of quarantining during epidemics placing medical care within a larger ethos of Jewish law, social welfare and public health. Jewish attitudes towards the body have been largely positive affirming the body as sacred and a carrier of the will of God.

Jewish attitudes towards physicians when they developed within the Greek world were also generally positive. The Talmud counseled Jews not to live in a city that did not have physicians who were understood as operating within the larger framework of Jewish law. Because a significant part of the Greek medical tradition was rationalistic this allowed Jews to separate out the techniques from their religious elements.

Jews often worked in collaboration with Muslims and Christians and were active in preserving and creating works on medicine. Jewish physicians were prominent in the teaching of medicine and in advancing the works of Hippocrates and Galen.

Influential rabbi Joseph Caro (1488–1575 CE) wrote that the Torah gave permission to the physician to heal. This work was seen as being in direct alignment with the religious value of saving and protecting life. The actions of the physician were viewed as cooperating with the will of God. In the medieval Jewish world, it was common for a person to fulfill the role of both rabbi and physician.

Service to God and community are understood as being linked and acts of care were seen as contributing to perfecting and repairing the world (*tikkun olam*). Attempting to cure someone of an ailment was seen as an expression of the ethical teachings of the tradition and considered a *miizvot*, both a divine commandment and a blessing.

Maimonides, Jewish rabbi and physician (1135–1204 CE), is a paradigmatic figure within Judaism and is considered one of the most important philosophers in the western world. He combined a humanistic world view with theological and philosophical insights drawing on Jewish sacred texts and the works of Plato and Aristotle. His great work *Guide for the Perplexed* is considered to be a classic of world literature.

Maimonides is also emblematic of the larger forces shaping the Jewish community as he was forced to flee his home in Cordoba, Spain as persecutions against Jews in Spain became more extreme. Maimonides went on to become physician to Sultan Saladin in Egypt. According to Maimonides, all of Jewish law aims at two things: the improvement of the body and the improvement of the soul. Maimonides stated that in caring for the physical one would have a "sound body with which to serve God".

From the holistic perspective presented by Maimonides both the soul and the body can become diseased. Health, in all senses of the word requires a moral life based in Jewish law. He taught that, "it is impossible to love God and achieve the highest levels of concentration if one is sick, undisciplined and living in fear of bodily harm" (Seeskin, 2021). The understanding of the particular ethical implications of the practice of medicine were recognized by Maimonides and expressed with the oath associated with him.

## *The Oath of Maimonides, the Physician's Prayer (excerpt)*

The eternal providence has appointed me to watch over the life and health of Thy creatures. May the love of my art actuate me all times; may neither avarice nor miserliness, nor thirst for glory or for a great reputation engage my mind; for the enemies of truth and philanthropy could easily deceive me and make me forget my lofty aim of doing good to Thy children.

May I never see the patient anything but a fellow creature in pain. Grant me the strength, time and opportunity always to correct what I have acquired, always to extend its domain; for knowledge is immense and the spirit of man can extend and indefinitely enrich itself daily with new requirements.

Today we can discover his errors of yesterday and tomorrow he can obtain a new light on what he thinks himself sure of today. Oh God, Thou has appointed me to watch over life and death of Thy creatures; here am I ready for my vocation and now I turn unto my calling.

—Jewish Virtual Library, Fordham University

## JEWISH COMMUNITY MEDICINE

Throughout the Middle Ages, Jews in Europe were active as physicians and in teaching medicine at the newly founded universities of Montpellier in France and in Bologna, Italy. Jewish hospitals were built beginning in the 18th century in western and central Europe. Guttman and Wright (2018) note that the building of Jewish hospitals resulted from the desire to provide health care within a Jewish framework that would allow serving kosher food but also as a reaction to anti-Semitism (p. 3).

Whether in the colonies of Palestine in the 19th century that would later become Israel, or in North America and Europe medicine in a Jewish context reflected cultural and religious values. Communities in Europe were concerned with facilitating Jewish communal life as prescribed by Jewish law (*halakha*).

Doctors were and are greatly respected for their efforts to benefit the community. However, even at this early stage, Jewish doctors were struggling to resolve issues related to patients' rights, informed consent, confidentiality, or speaking the truth to a patient. The idea of the doctor remaining under public scrutiny and a servant of the community remained a central idea within these communities. The medical system that developed in Israel reflected the values of: 1. Sanctity of Human Life; 2. Primacy of Jewish Law; 3. Medicine under Society's Scrutiny (Navot, 2003, p. 52).

Jewish community medicine emphasized equality and justice for all, and the right to receive medical treatment without discrimination. The poor as well as the rich were granted treatment, according to Jewish concepts of social justice. Each clinic had office hours for poor patients, and a special fee for house calls.

In the diaspora Jewish hospitals developed in order to provide for the specific needs of Jewish communities. These needs included kosher food and a culturally sensitive environment. These hospitals also provided a space where Jewish doctors could train (Guttman and Wright, 2018, p. 7).

Mount Sinai Hospital, New York City, one of the most renowned hospitals in the world, was founded in 1852 by nine men representing a variety of Jewish charities. They shared a commitment to provide free medical care for Jews in need in New York City. In 1855, that vision came to fruition with the establishment of the 45-bed hospital in what was then a rural neighbourhood on West 28th Street between Seventh and Eighth Avenues.

Although the hospital was a sectarian institution, the hospital accepted emergency patients of any religious affiliation. In its first years of operation, the majority of patients were foreign born. As the hospital was a charitable enterprise, its directors relied on the gifts of friends and members and payments from the government were used to subsidize care.

In Montreal, responding to the needs of a rapidly growing Jewish community, a hospital was founded in 1934. The creation of the hospital came about through the fundraising efforts of the women of the community. The fundraisers recognized the anti-Semitism that was a feature of medical education across Canada.

The hospital was open to all patients, regardless of race, religion, language, or ethnic background. Emerging from its roots as a small community institution, the Jewish General Hospital in Montreal is now a major component of McGill University's medical school and carries out 22% of the training at the McGill Faculty of Medicine.

Even within a scientific and research driven paradigm these hospitals have retained their sense of purpose. The mission statement of the Sinai Health states: "From our two founding institutions comes the belief that we are here in service of others. Our shared history of caring for those who were vulnerable and marginalized, and our Jewish heritage calls us to serve the health needs of our community".

## HEALING VERSUS CURING: CONTEMPORARY JUDAISM AND HEALTH

Former director of Harvard's Religion, Health and Healing Initiative (RHHI) Susan Sered notes that the Jewish American community accepted and adopted the biomedical model perhaps more than any other community. The whole-hearted embracing of this approach in North America resulted in very little in the way of religious approaches to healing until the 1980s.

The Jewish Healing movement emerged alongside the larger alternative healing movement in the western world which was strongly influenced by the feminist movement. The ordination of women rabbis resulted in many of these women taking leadership in new approaches to Judaism and healing. The Jewish Healing Movement recognizes its hybrid origins and has adopted features from within the larger holistic health movement within a Jewish framework of understanding and practice.

Many of the newer forms of Jewish healing are critical of notions of physical perfectibility and the tendency to see illness as a failure. Instead, this approach recognizes the vulnerability of the human condition and reframes it as a potentially spiritual experience. Part of this framing is recognition that illness and mortality are unavoidable parts of the human experience.

Emphasizing the difference between curing and healing is an important aspect of the Jewish approach to health. These healing methodologies were never intended to replace biomedical treatment. Curing, from this perspective is associated strictly with the physical while healing takes in many other dimensions of the human person. As an informant told Sered (2005), "It isn't always possible to cure, but it is always possible to heal" (p. 234).

This understanding of healing takes into account the totality of a human life and not just the state of the physical body. As Rabbi Nancy Flam (2005) put it:

> Healing is a sense of wholeness, perspective, reintegration, and not the removal of a tumour or clearing of infection.... It addresses the dimension of the person that was suffering and not just the disease.
>
> *(ibid p. 235)*

These practices mitigate the often-alienating environments of many health clinics and hospitals emphasizing the importance and individuality of each patient.

There is a recognition within the Jewish healing movement that one's entire identity can become subsumed within the illness and constant medical visits and treatments. Religious healing rituals are a way of reasserting the identity of the sick person beyond their physical condition and the often-depersonalizing aspects of biomedicine.

These practices allow the individual to live in "Jewish time" rather than simply being controlled by institutional schedules of the hospital. Reasserting the individuality and meaning of each life can be a profound part of the healing process.

Jewish approaches to health and healing also engage with the larger issue of mortality and that "a true healing may be a death" (Sered, 2005, p. 237). The use of midrash and traditional approaches of study and reflection are part of supporting those who are experiencing illness and the effects of aging. The religious text can be used as a resource for reflection on the challenges facing oneself and one's family. Supporting the family of the person who is ill is also highlighted in contemporary Jewish pastoral care.

All approaches recognize that God is the power at work and as Rabbi Amy Eilberg states "we want to remember that God is the Healer and the ways of God's healing are far more mysterious than we can know and predict" (ibid. p. 245). Practices may include intercessory prayer based on the model of Numbers 12:1–15 in which the High Priest, Aaron, asks Moses to pray for their sister Miriam. In other rituals Shekhinah, the indwelling spirit, is called upon.

In her ethnographic study of members of a Jewish community in Arizona, Gila Silverman looked at the healing practice of *the Mi Sheberach* prayer. Silverman found that the prayer was being used in both a traditional and modernized form in synagogues, homes, hospitals, and healing circles. She concluded that the prayer which has deep emotional resonance regardless of levels of religiosity, contributes to a feeling of agency, and to aid in a sense of connection to both the people praying and the person experiencing illness.

Silverman (2016) describes the way in which prayer bypasses the intellect and speaks to the emotions of those experiencing sickness. She also notes that when a name is read aloud during a synagogue service it also mobilizes the friends and community who may have not known the person was ill. She quotes an informant who was going through cancer treatment and had considered herself a secular Jew as saying, "Everyone is praying for me the Jews, the Catholics, the Buddhists. –I'll take it all" (p. 175).

The Jewish healing movement has also addressed how those working in the fields of medicine can integrate their tradition with their vocation. In discussing spiritual resources for those working in health care, Elizabeth Feldman (2013) offers a variety of ways that their faith can support them in their professions. This can include a traditional purification prayer while hand washing before surgery, centring practices, meditation, and social justice work.

The larger Jewish tradition guides both the one seeking healing and those supporting them in how to act with compassion and as a community. Influenced by contemporary alternative health movements these approaches have continued to evolve while maintaining their essentially Jewish character.

> May the one who blessed our ancestors, Abraham, Isaac and Jacob, Sarah, Rebecca and Leah, bless and heal those who are ill (names). May the Blessed Holy One be filled with compassion for their health to be restored and their strength to be revived. May God swiftly send them a complete renewal of body and spirit. And let us say, Amen.
>
> From *Mishkan HaNeFesh for Youth*, copyright 2018 by the Central Conference of American Rabbis.

## REFLECTION

1. Why do you think a distinction is made between healing and curing in the Jewish healing movement?
2. How can religion and culture contribute to maintaining a sense of self in the face of illness and treatment?
3. Why do you think public scrutiny of doctors is such an important idea in the Jewish understanding of biomedicine? Do you agree?

## OVERVIEW OF JUDAISM

Belief in the Revelation of God's will through Prophets, the most important being Moses.

The sanctity of human life and the ethical imperative to preserve it.

Estimated number of followers: 15.7 million.

The Ten Commandments: These are the first ten of the 613 commandments given by God to the Jewish people. They form the foundation of Jewish ethics, behaviour, and responsibility.

1) I am the Lord thy god, who brought thee out of the land of Egypt, out of the house of bondage.
2) Thou shalt have no other gods before Me.
3) Thou shalt not take the name of the Lord thy God in vain.
4) Remember the Sabbath day to keep it holy.
5) Honor thy father and thy mother.
6) Thou shalt not murder.
7) Thou shalt not commit adultery.
8) Thou shalt not steal.
9) Thou shalt not bear false witness against thy neighbour.
10) Thou shalt not covet anything that belongs to thy neighbour.

Key Figures: Abraham, the first Patriarch, Moses who is believed to have led his community out of captivity and received the Ten Commandments on Mount Sinai.

Holy City: Jerusalem

Liturgical Language: Hebrew

Scriptures: Tanakh: Torah, Nebi'im (Prophets), Kethubah (writings) Mishnah (understood as codification of oral law), Talmud (commentaries on the Mishanh), Midrash (interpretation of Biblical texts centred on moral principles and law).

Main Divisions:

Orthodox, Conservative, Reform, Reconstructionist, Hassidism.

Institutions: In the earliest communities the Temple at Jerusalem and after the destruction of the Temple in 70 CE the synagogue became the gathering place for services and ritual.

Religious Specialists: After the destruction of the Temple the function of the priest was replaced by the rabbi, a teacher expert on interpreting the Torah, conducting rituals and leader of the community or congregation. Jewish chaplains often serve within hospital settings.

Beliefs Regarding the Afterlife: Generally not clear as emphasis is on an ethically lived life.

Many Jewish communities have access to a *chevra kadisha* (burial society) that prepare the body for burial according to Jewish tradition.

Sitting Shiva is a traditional seven-day practice in which the bereaved family receives visitors and generally the community provides for their needs during this time.

## REFERENCES

I am the Lord Your Healer, Exodus 15:26 KJ21.

Feldman, Elizabeth. (2013). Spiritual Resources for Jewish Healthcare Professionals. *Judaism and Health. A Handbook of Practical, Professional and Scholarly Resources*. Jewish Lights Publishing.

Guttman, Frank Myron and Alexander Wright. (2018). *The Sir Mortimer B Davis Jewish General Hospital*. McGill-Queen's Press.

Navot, Orit. (2003). A Historical Overview of the Developing Medical Ethics Culture in the New Jewish Settlement in Israel During the Years 1840–1914. *Eubios Journal of Asian and International Bioethics*, 13, 52–3.

Seeskin, Kenneth. (Spring 2021). Maimonides. *The Stanford Encyclopedia of Philosophy*, Edward N. Zalta (Ed.). https://plato.stanford.edu/entries/maimonides/

Sered, Susan. (2005). Healing as Resistance. Reflections Upon New Forms of Jewish American Healing. *Religion and Healing in America*. Linda L. Barnes and Susan Sered (Eds.). Oxford University Press.

Silverman, Gila S. (July 2016). "I'll Say a Mi Sheberach for You." Prayer, Healing and Identity Among Liberal American Jews. *Contemporary Jewry*, 36 (2), 169–85.

Springer, Rabbi Mychal B. (2013). Jewish Pastoral Care. *Judaism and Health. A Handbook of Practical, Professional and Scholarly Resources*. Jewish Lights Publishing.

## FURTHER READING

Ben-Arye, Eran, Khaled Karkabi, Sonia Karkabi, Yael Keshet, Maria Haddad, and Moshe Frenkel. (2009). Attitudes of Arab and Jewish Patients toward Integration of Complementary Medicine in Primary Care Clinics in Israel: A Cross-cultural Study. *Social Science and Medicine*, 68 (1), 177–82.

Bleich, David J. (1981/2002). *Judaism and Healing. Halakhic Perspectives*. Ktav Publishing House.

Cutter, Rabbi William and Ronald M. Andiman. (2013). Words Worth Healing. *Judaism and Health. A Handbook of Practical, Professional and Scholarly Resources*. Jewish Lights Publishing.

Freedman, Benjamin. (1990). Duty and Healing. Foundations of Jewish Bioethics. *Medicine and Jewish Law. Volume One*. Fred Rosner (Ed.). Jason Aronson Publishers.

Freeman, David. (2005). Healing and Medicine in Judaism. *Encyclopedia of Religion*, 6, 3828–31.

*Healing and the Jewish Imagination: Spiritual and Practical Perspectives on Judaism and Health*. (2007). William Cutter (Ed.). Jewish Lights Publishing.

*Healing of Soul, Healing of Body: Spiritual Leaders Unfold Their Strength and Solace in Psalms*. (1994). Rabbi Simkha Y. Weintraub (Ed.). Jewish Lights Publishing.

Hirsh, Rabbi Richard. (2003). Reflections on "Healing" in Contemporary Liberal Judaism. *The Mitzvah of Healing. An Anthology of Jewish Texts, Meditations, Essays, Personal Stories and Ritual*s. Hara Person (Ed.). UAHC.

Isaacs, Ronald H. (1998). *Judaism, Medicine and Healing*. Jason Aronson Publishers.

Jacobs, Louis. (1997). The Body in Jewish Worship: Three Rituals Examined. *Religion and the Body*. Sarah Coakley (Ed.). Cambridge University Press.

*Judaism and Health. A Handbook of Practical, Professional and Scholarly Resources*. (2013). Jeffrey S. Levin and Michele F. Prince (Eds.). Woodstock. Jewish Lights Publishing.

Lev, Efraim and Zohar Amar. (2006). Reconstruction of the Inventory of Material Medica used by Members of the Jewish Community of Medieval Cairo According to Prescriptions Found in the Taylor-Schechter Genizah Collection. *Journal of Ethnopharmacology*, 108 (3), 428–44.

Lever, Aaron M. (2001). *Guide Me Along the Way. A Jewish Spiritual Companion for Surgery*. National Center for Jewish Healing.

Levin, Jeffrey. (2013). Religion and Mental Health Among Israeli Jews: Findings From the SHARE_Israel Study. *Social Indicators Research*, 113 (3), 769–84.

Levin, Jeffrey and Michele F. Prince. (December 2011). Judaism and Health: Reflections on An Emerging Scholarly Field. *Journal of Religion and Health*, 50 (4), 765–77.

Mark, Naomi. (2003). A Perspective on Jewish Healing. *The Mitzvah of Healing. An Anthology of Jewish Texts, Meditations, Essays, Personal Stories and Ritual*s. Hara Person (Ed.). UAHC.

McCallum, Donald. (2007). *Maimonides' Guide for the Perplexed: Silence And Salvation*. Routledge.

*Medicine and Jewish Law. Volume One*. (1990). Fred Rosner (Ed.). Jason Aronson Publishers.

Meri, Josef. (2016). Medicine: The Reception and Practice of Rationalist Medicine and Thought in Medieval Jewish Communities, East and West. *The Routledge Handbook of Muslim-Jewish Relations*. Routledge.

*Midrash Medicine. Healing Body and Soul in the Jewish Interpretative Tradition.* (2011). Rabbi William Cutter (Ed.). Jewish Lights Publishing.

Praglin, Laura J. (2003). The Jewish Healing Tradition in Historical Perspective. *The Mitzvah of Healing. An Anthology of Jewish Texts, Meditations, Essays, Personal Stories and Rituals*. Hara Person (Ed.). UAHC.

Prince, Michele F. (Summer/Fall 2009). Judaism, Health, and Healing: How a New Jewish Communal Field Took Root and Where it Might Grow. *Journal of Jewish Communal Service*, 84 (3/4), 280–91.

Rosner, Fred. (1972). *Modern Medicine and Jewish Law*. Yeshiva University.

Rubenfire, Adam. (2017). Jewish Hospitals Keep Traditions Alive After Mergers. *Modern Healthcare*, (October 7, 2017).

Ruderman, David B. (2001). *Jewish Thought and Scientific Discovery in Early Modern Europe*. Wayne State University Press. Originally published in 1995.

Sharabi, Asaf. (April 2014). Deep Healing: Ritual Healing in the Teshuvah Movement. *Anthropology and Medicine*, 21 (3), 1–13.

Spitzer, Joseph. (2003). *Caring for Jewish Patients*. CRC Press.

Szmerla, Rephoel. (2017). *Alternative Medicine in Halachah*. Israel Bookshop Publications.

## INTERNET RESOURCES

Jewish Health Organization: https://jho.org/

Kalsman Institute on Judaism and Health: http://kalsman.huc.edu/

Mission Statement Sinai Health: https://www.sinaihealth.ca/about-sinai-health/our-vision-mission-purpose-and-values/

The Mount Sinai Hospital: https://www.mountsinai.org/locations/mount-sinai

# 9 Proclaim the Kingdom and Heal the Sick: Christianity and Healing

Christianity developed from the teachings and life example of Jesus of Nazareth in 1st-century Palestine, then part of the Roman Empire. Believed by Christians to be the Messiah, Jesus emphasized the coming of a New Age characterized by justice, mercy, and peace. Jesus' teaching gained followers throughout the Jewish world and then beyond eventually becoming a separate tradition that is now international in scope with over 1.5 billion followers.

The central tenets of Christianity hold that Jesus was both man and God but the intricacies of the doctrine developed into various streams within the tradition. These include Greek Orthodox, Roman Catholic, Protestant, Evangelical, and Pentecostal. The Christian Churches also developed a monastic tradition that included both men and women who, as monks and nuns, left worldly life behind taking vows of poverty, chastity, and obedience.

After Christianity became the religion of the Roman empire under the emperor Constantine in the 4th century CE, its institutions developed rapidly with the building of churches, development of liturgy, and pilgrimage routes. Until the coming of modernity in the 17th century, Christian values infused western society with ideas about limits on wealth and lending money and the need to provide for the vulnerable. Like the other Abrahamic religions of Judaism and Islam there is a strong emphasis on ethical conduct and social welfare.

The centrality of healing within the Christian tradition was established by its founder. According to the Gospels of the New Testament, wherever Jesus went the sick were brought to him to be healed and he exhorted his followers to do the same. This practice was one of the key ways in which his teachings were spread and attested to his authority as a spiritual leader and messiah. Over time Christianity

DOI: 10.4324/9781003471769-9

developed into many different streams and denominations but healing has remained a central part of all of them. This continues into the present in a wide variety of practices and institutions including: prayer, laying on of hands, healing circles, healing shrines, building of hospitals and hospices, and medical nursing orders.

Throughout the Christian Gospels Jesus is described as healing people of both physical and mental ailments. One of the many examples appears in Matthew 15:29–31 which states:

> After Jesus left that place, he passed along the Sea of Galilee, and he went up the mountain and sat down. Great crowds came to him, bringing with them the lame, the maimed, the blind, the mute, and many others. They put them at his feet and he cured them.

At least 42 cases of healing are mentioned specifically in the Christian scripture. Jesus is described as healing both mental and physical illness mostly by touch and through commands, and, in some cases, people were healed merely by touching his garments.

In some of the accounts in the New Testament Jesus emphasizes faith as being necessary for healing but at other times he does not. Faith might also be demonstrated of behalf of another. In the Gospel of Mark Jesus says to the father of a sick child, "If you can believe, all things are possible to him who believes." Immediately the father of the child cried out and said with tears, "Lord, I believe; help my unbelief!" (Mark 9:23–25).

In some cases, forgiveness of sin is highlighted as is recounted in John 5:14 where Jesus tells a man that he has been healed and, "Sin no more that nothing worse will befall you". However, this connection between ethical behaviour and wellness is only highlighted in a minority of the gospels. In the majority of cases Jesus is described as healing spontaneously and out of compassion.

## *Matthew 9:20–22*

And suddenly, a woman who had a flow of blood for twelve years came from behind and touched the hem of His garment. For she said to herself, "If only I may touch His garment, I shall be made well". But Jesus turned around, and when He saw her He said, "Be of good cheer, daughter; your faith has made you well". And the woman was made well from that hour.

As the institutions and liturgy of Christianity developed, healing remained a central concern. The theological underpinnings of these practices evolved from the example of Jesus and his disciples and from the principles of compassion, hospitality, and care for the stranger, widow, and orphan. The tale of the Good Samaritan is another example from scripture often cited as a warrant for healing and care. This narrative emphasizes care for others regardless of their cultural or religious background.

The healing tradition can be seen in all branches of Christianity in the figure of charismatic healers, healing rituals, sacred healing centres (Kinsley, 1996, p. 96). Throughout the Christian world all include prayers for the sick within the liturgy each Sunday. Congregants send in names of friends or relatives who are ill and they are read out and prayed for during the service.

The laying on of hands is another practice common across the Christian tradition. In the New Testament the ideas drawn from Judaism of consecration and transmission are present. The New Testament further indicates that the imposition of hands conveyed a blessing and was a means of healing. Many Christian churches have prayer and healing networks and rituals such as prayer and laying on of hands may be practiced by the laity as as group or by the clergy or both. It continues to be a typical practice that certain women noted for their piousness in a community are given lists of names for whom they pray.

Various regional traditions developed within Christianity as different communities developed their own saints many of whom were associated with healing Prayers for healing could also be addressed to a saint in the Catholic tradition or to the archangels. An example is prayers for healing to Padre Pio in Italy or Brother Andre in Canada who were healers and are now canonized within the Catholic tradition.

There are also saints associated with the healing of specific illnesses such as St Peregrine as the patron saint of cancer. Various saints also became associated with health and healing including St Brigid, Patroness of healing and Saint Catherine of Sienna, patron saint of nursing.

The Christian tradition has many healing shrines and sites that attract pilgrims seeking healing. Lourdes is the pre-eminent site of healing pilgrimage in the Roman Catholic tradition welcoming millions of visitors each year (see Appendix 2). There are also important shrines in Portugal, Eastern Europe, and in Quebec such as St. Anne de Beaupre and the Oratory of St Joseph in Montreal, Quebec. The Oratory welcomes over a million pilgrims a year.

Healing rituals at these shrines include bathing in holy water, attending masses, making votive offerings, saying prayers and writing petitions. The material culture of these sites are extremely important and include holy water and oil. This, in turn, can be brought back and given to friends and family emphasizing social solidarity and care for those who are sick.

On an institutional level, from the earliest days of the church, Christians created a variety of spaces to care for the sick and destitute. Christian women in the early communities such as St Fabiola in Rome set up spaces in her own home to care for those in need. She used her large family fortune to establish a general public hospital in Rome and attended the sick herself. Monasteries were also often the site of infirmaries which were precursors of hospitals.

Two of the first free standing hospitals in Europe were the Hotel Dieu founded in Lyon in 542 CE and the Hotel Dieu in Paris founded in 660 CE. Christianity has remained intertwined the building and staffing of hospitals from its founding into the present. The concepts of love (*charitas*) and suffering/frailty (*infirmitas*) led to the building of hospitals, hostels, and hospices throughout the Christian world. The building of these institutions was understood as embodying the obligation to love and care for one's neighbour and were understood as a being an imitation of the healing and compassionate mission of the Jesus and an embodiment of Christian values.

## CHRISTIAN ATTITUDES TO THE BODY

Christianity evolving as it did from Judaism adopted the Jewish emphasis upon the sanctity of life and reverence for the human body. The influence of the Greek philosophical traditions tended to emphasize the importance of the soul over the body. While the tradition differs slightly in the branches of Orthodox, Roman Catholic, and Protestant the overall attitude was one of ambivalence. Kallistos (1997) Ware sums up the Greek Orthodox attitude in the sayings of John Climacus of the 7th century who said of his body, "He is my helper, my assistant and my opponent, a protector and a traitor" (p. 90).

The reason for this mixed assessment is the freight the body carries in terms of its association with sins such as lust and gluttony and so on one hand can be viewed as a hindrance in the spiritual life. Alternately the body is seen as an essential part of one's personhood and as created by God, and therefore good.

In the contemporary period the Christian tradition has tended to emphasize a more positive attitude towards the body. This approach draws on the scriptural description of the body as the "temple of God". This, then, calls for respectful care of one's own body and the bodies of others. From a Christian perspective care of the body was seen as concomitant with care of the soul.

## NURSING THE WHOLE PERSON: THE CONNECTION BETWEEN NURSING AND CHRISTIANITY

The practice of nursing reaches as far back in time as can traced in the historical record and in fact begins with the care that a mother gives an infant. The word itself derives from the idea of nurture. The figure of the nurse appears throughout the historical records in Mesopotamia, Egypt and Greece, but the clearest lineage for nurses in the western world emerges from the Christian tradition. Christianity emphasized the dignity of each individual life and took the parable of the Good Samaritan as an instruction to tend to the well-being of any person in need. Each act of charity from this view was of value and done for Christ who was to be seen in each person. The roots of both nursing and social work can be seen as emerging from this worldview.

The earliest forms of nursing within Christianity were viewed as a form of Christian charity in action. The earliest mention appears within the very first Christian communities in the 1st century CE in the form of deaconesses whose role was to distribute alms to poor and attend to the sick. The term is drawn from the Greek *diaokonen* meaning "to serve" and also gave name to early precursors of hospitals called *diakonias* as Christians opened their homes to those in need.

In their position serving the community the deaconesses were forerunners of community health nurses and social workers. The Corporeal Works of Mercy that deaconesses were to perform were as follows:

To feed the hungry

To give water to the thirsty

To clothe the naked

To visit the imprisoned

To shelter the homeless

To care for the sick

To bury the dead.

*(Matthew 23:35–46)*

These acts are based on the 25th chapter of Matthew in the New Testament and the *Book of Isaiah* in the Hebrew Bible. These emphasize the concrete actions that must be taken alongside spiritual belief. In attending to those in need, including sick members of the community, the deaconesses performed a variety of functions including: feeding, bathing, dressing wounds, giving medicine, and providing spiritual counsel.

Within Roman society wealthy women who had converted to Christianity became known as matrons and many founded both hospitals and convents. In the 4th century CE, St. Helena, the mother of the Emperor Constantine who made the Roman Empire Christian, was known to have given money to the poor and to have founded a home for the aged. St Marcella was another wealthy Roman woman who converted to Christianity and turned her home into a monastery. She studied and taught Greek, Latin, and Hebrew and is sometimes looked upon as the first nurse educator.

Another approach to health care was developed when the order of the Knights Hospitaller of St John was founded as military nursing order during the period of the Crusades beginning in the 11th century CE. The men wore their robes over suits of armor emblazoned with a Maltese cross that is now the symbol of the International Red Cross. Throughout the Middle Ages monasteries and convents often functioned medical centres. Hospices were opened up along the pilgrimage routes from Europe to Palestine serving the various physical needs of pilgrims including health care.

In the 16th century more than 100 female religious orders specializing in nursing were founded. Among the earliest settlers to New France, Jeanne Mance established the first hospital and brought over members of the Sisters of St Joseph to staff the new institution. These nuns were instrumental in the building of hospitals and developing medical programmes throughout North America.

These nursing orders were part of far-reaching international networks and so could be sent to wherever they were needed including Canada, the US, and Australia throughout the 19th century. With the coming of the industrial revolution the plight of the urban poor came to the fore and nursing began to take shape as a profession.

## FLORENCE NIGHTINGALE: A NEW MODEL OF NURSING

It is impossible to over-estimate the influence of Florence Nightingale (1820–1910) on the development of nursing. Nightingale was a social reformer who advocated for the profession of nursing and public health as part of her desire to create a better society. She was motivated by deeply held religious convictions and her concern for social welfare resulted in the creation of nursing as a profession, and influenced the ways in which hospitals were built and the concept of holistic health.

Nightingale was born into a wealthy English family in which it was socially unacceptable for women to work. In 1837 at age 16 she underwent a religious conversion and experienced a call to service. However, it wasn't until 1851 that she received permission from her father to begin undertaking the work that would make her admired around the world.

While born and remaining within the Church of England, Nightingale held many unorthodox religious opinions. She saw her role as being "God's co-worker" and this meant using all the most contemporary tools at her disposal including statistics and research. She was clear that nursing training was to be non-sectarian and not a branch of a missionary work. Her writings on nursing are practical and focus on sanitation, fresh air, observation, and light. Nonetheless, she retained a religious outlook throughout her life stating that, "I don't think any words had a fuller possession of my mind through life than Christ's putting himself in the place of the sick, the infirm, the prisoner" (quoted in McDonald, 2001, p. 20).

Nightingale began her training at the (Protestant) Deaconess Institution in Kaiserswerth Germany and then with Roman Catholic nursing orders in Paris in 1853. Her work during the Crimean War made her famous as the "Lady with the Lamp". She took a cobbled together group of women to serve that included members of the Irish Sisters of Mercy. Returning to England she founded the first institution for teaching nursing and this soon spread throughout the western world. Her letters reveal that she was an indefatigable advocate for the evolving profession of nursing defending the rights of nurses to proper accommodation, food, and payment.

Nightingale's theory of nursing emphasized treating the person and not the disease and placed a great deal of importance on fresh air, cleanliness and proper diet. Her idea of nursing divided it into four primary domains: biological, psychological, social and spiritual.

As a result, nursing from its inception into the present has been an "integrative healing discipline" (Koithan, 2018, p. 3).

> Surgery removes the bullet out of the limb, which is an obstruction to cure, but nature heals the wound. So it is with medicine; the function of an organ becomes obstructed, medicine so far as we know, assists nature to remove the obstruction; but does nothing more. And what nursing has to do in either case, is to put the patient in the best condition for nature to act upon him.
>
> Florence Nightingale, *Notes on Nursing*, 1860. p. 191

## HEALTH AND HEALING IN THE AFRICAN AMERICAN CHURCHES

The impact of religion on health, both mental and physical, is illustrated very clearly by the African American churches of the United States. From their inception historically black churches have played a vital role in supporting the well-being of communities. The narratives of Exodus served to shore up the self-esteem and hope of enslaved communities and served as a code for those seeking freedom. The churches were organizers of the Underground Railway and the key players in the Civil Rights movement and continue to support community welfare into the present. Attending to a congregation's health from this perspective is part of a larger project of community well-being and represents an "active, powerful, creative partnership with God" (Michem, 2005, p. 279).

Religious belief and practice have played a vital role in protecting the community against the dehumanizing influences of racism and continues to provide concrete mental and physical supports. Based on the scriptures and beliefs common to all Christians the African American churches, developed their own patterns of worship and institutions adapted to their own culture and needs. Within this worldview the well-being of the whole community is emphasized alongside that of the individual.

The psychologically protective function of the African American churches contributed to creating what Davis-Carroll (2011) calls an "ethic of resistance". This support for both physical and mental health is created by language, music, rhetoric that emphasizes the value of all human beings, and liberatory practices of storytelling and sharing that emphasize resilience and agency. Researchers also note the way that the churches have created a bulwark against the pathologizing of black bodies emphasizing the importance and sacredness of each human being.

In their study of the websites of predominantly black megachurches in the southeastern US, Campbell and Wallace (2015) found that 74% mentioned a general health ministry. These churches addressed the needs of those suffering from illnesses such as cancer, HIV/AIDs, addiction, and diabetes. Their holistic approach emphasized mind, body, and spirit and often included emotional and financial well- being within the ambit of their concerns.

Looking at the influence of church participation on women Michem (2005) writes that, "Lived in the body, community and the world, African American women's faith often extends to hope for healing of all people as a natural corollary of envisioning a new, more perfect world" (281). Belief and practice offer both inspiration and concrete support for community members. Many of the churches sponsor clinics, workshops, and access to information as part of church activities.

Many of the churches have also cooperated with government agencies to bridge mental health supports to African American communities. These alliances work with the historical recognition of medical racism epitomized in the notorious US government-funded Tuskegee Syphilis Study that ran from 1932 to 1972. As a trusted social institutions black churches have been able to effectively bridge health care to their communities.

## *Healing Prayers*

### For a Sick Person

O Father of mercies and God of all comfort, our only help in time of need: We humbly beseech thee to behold, visit, and relieve thy sick servant *N.* for whom our prayers are desired. Look upon *him* with the eyes of thy mercy; comfort *him* with a sense of thy goodness; preserve *him* from the temptations of the enemy; and give *him* patience under *his* affliction. In thy good time, restore *him* to health, and enable *him* to lead the residue of *his* life in thy fear, and to thy glory; and grant that finally *he* may dwell with thee in life everlasting; through Jesus Christ our Lord. *Amen.*

## For Recovery from Sickness

O God, the strength of the weak and the comfort of sufferers: Mercifully accept our prayers, and grant to your servant *N.* the help of your power, that *his* sickness may be turned into health, and our sorrow into joy; through Jesus Christ our Lord. *Amen.*

## For a Sick Child

Heavenly Father, watch with us over your child *N.*, and grant that *he* may be restored to that perfect health which it is yours alone to give; through Jesus Christ our Lord. *Amen.*

## Before an Operation

Almighty God our heavenly Father, graciously comfort your servant *N.* in *his* suffering, and bless the means made use of for *his* cure. Fill *his* heart with confidence that, though at times *he* may be afraid, *he* yet may put *his* trust in you; through Jesus Christ our Lord. *Amen.*

—*The Book of Common Prayer*

# *Community Care and Mental Health: The Example of Geel*

For 700 years the community of Geel, Belgium has hosted those experiencing mental health challenges. Geel has been called the oldest continuous community mental healthcare system in the world. The church in Geel, which is dedicated to St Dymphna, patron saint of mental illness, has long attracted pilgrims experiencing mental illness.

As a result of the influx of pilgrims to Geel beginning in the medieval period, the townspeople began a practice of lodging the visitors which has continued into the present. In this community-wide effort each boarder is first interviewed by the health authority and then placed with a host. The Belgian government has oversight of the programme offers a small payment to those who act as foster families. Service to the boarders includes care by a psychiatrist, psychologist, nurse, and social worker and Geel has been described as a "hospital without walls".

The Geel community models community-based care and "acceptance of mental differences" (Chen 2016). This lack of stigma and sense of hope is a vital part of the efficacy of the practices. The emphasis is not on curing but on caring and the idea that entire community looks out for the well-being of the people who have moved to Geel for support.

Geel has long been recognized for the success of its model and has inspired imitation all over the world. With the deinstitutionalization movement in mental health in the 1960s and 1970s many recognized that former patients would require support in order to find their place in society. While the approaches to therapeutic communities differs according to different situations and resources all share what Goldstein (2003) refers to as the "spirit of St Dymphna" (p. 113).

Ellen Baxter, an American psychology student, spent a year in Geel to observe the community. Inspired by what she experienced she went on to found Broadway Housing Communities (BHC) in 1983 in New York city. The organization, galvanized by the issue of homelessness and poverty, has developed integrated affordable housing for those who need it. These residences offer medical, mental health, addiction, and employment support.

## OVERVIEW OF CHRISTIANITY

Founded *c.* 3 BCE–30 CE by Jesus of Nazareth and his Apostles.

Estimated Number of Followers: 1.5 billion.

Holy Cities: Jerusalem; for Roman Catholics, Rome.

Scripture: The Christian Bible includes the Old (Hebrew Bible) and New Testament, Roman Catholics hold the teaching office (*magisterium*) of the Church to be authoritative.

Key Texts: Hebrew Bible and New Testament.

Main Divisions: Roman Catholic, Orthodox, Protestant.

Religious Specialists: Roman Catholics (priest), Protestants (minister, pastor), deacons, monks, nuns, chaplains.

Belief in God as Trinity—God, Son, and Holy Spirit.

Rituals: The Eucharist a ceremonial meal of bread and wine commemorating the Last Supper of Jesus and his disciples; the Christian sacrament including baptism and marriage, individual and collective prayer; last rites performed by clergy leading up to or after death.

Beliefs regarding the Afterlife: Generally, a belief in divine judgement and heaven and hell (in some cases the intermediate state of purgatory).

Christians have traditionally practiced burial. This is changing particularly in North America and Europe where cremation is becoming a common practice.

## *The Nicene Creed (Christian Statement of Faith)*

I believe in one God, the Father almighty, maker of heaven and earth, of all things visible and invisible. I believe in one Lord Jesus Christ, the Only Begotten Son of God, Born of the Father before all ages. God from God, Light from Light, True God from true God, Begotten, not made, consubstantial with the Father; Through him all things were made. For us men and for our salvation He came down from heaven, And by the Holy Spirit was incarnate of the Virgin Mary, And became man. For our sake he was crucified under Pontius Pilate, He suffered death and was buried, And rose again on the third day In accordance with the Scriptures. He ascended into heaven And is seated at the right hand of the Father. He will come again in glory To judge the living and the dead And his kingdom will have no end. I believe in the Holy Spirit, the Lord, the giver of life, Who proceeds from the Father [and the Son], Who with the Father and the Son is adored and glorified, Who has spoken through the prophets. I believe in one, holy, catholic and apostolic Church. I confess one Baptism for the forgiveness of sins and I look forward to the resurrection of the dead. And the life of the world to come. Amen.

## REFERENCES

Proclaim the Kingdom and Heal the Sick, Luke 9:2.

Campbell, Anthony and Gail Wallace. (2015). Black Megachurch Websites: An Assessment of Health Content for Congregations and Communities. *Health Communication*, 30 (6), 557–65.

Chen, Andrew. For Centuries a Small Town Has Embraced Strangers With Mental Illness. NPR, July 1, 2016.

Davis-Carroll, Hilda R. (2011). An Ethic of Resistance: Choosing Health Messages for African American Women. *Journal of Religion and Health*, 50 (2), 219–31.

Florence Nightingale's Spiritual Journey. Biblical Annotations, Sermons and Journal Notes. (2001). *Collected Works. Volume 2*. Lynn McDonald (Ed.). Wilfrid Laurier University Press.

Goldstein, Jackie L. and Marc M. L. Godemont. (2003). The Legends and Lessons of Geel, Belgium: A 1500-Year-Old Legend, a 21st-Century Model. *Community Mental Health Journal*, 39, 441–58.

Kinsley, David. (1996). *Health, Healing and Religion: A Cross-Cultural Perspective*. Prentice Hall.

Koithan, Mary. (2018). Concepts and Principles of Integrative Nursing. *Integrative Nursing*. Second Edition. Mary Jo Kreitzer, Mary Koithan, and Andrew Weil (Eds.). Oxford University Press.

McDonald, Lynn. (2018). *Florence Nightingale. Nursing and Healthcare Today*. Springer Publishing.

Michem, Stephanie Y. (2005). "Jesus is My Doctor": Healing and Religion In African American Women's Lives. *Religion and Healing in America*. Linda L. Barnes and Susan S. Sered (Eds). Oxford University Press.

Nightingale, Florence. (1860.) *Notes on Nursing. What it Is and What It is Not*. Harrison and Sons.

Ware, Kalistos. (1997). 'My Helper and My Enemy': The Body In Greek Christianity. *Religion and the Body*. Sarah Coakley (Ed.). Cambridge University Press.

## FURTHER READING

Agrimi, Jole and Chiara Crisciani. (1998). Charity and Aid in Medieval Christian Civilization. *Western Medical Thought from Antiquity to the Middle Ages*. Edited by Mirko D. Grmek, translated by Mireille Muellner and Leonard Muellner. Harvard University Press.

Barrett-Lennard, R. (2005). The Canons of Hippolytus and Christian Concern With Illness, Health and Healing. *Journal of Early Christian Studies*, 13 (2), 137–64.

Bilsen, P. J. G. Henck. (August 2016). Lessons to be Learned from the Oldest Community Psychiatric Service in the World: Geel, Belgium. *British Journal of Psychiatry Bulletin*, 40, 207–11.

*Caregiving on the Periphery. Historical Perspectives on Nursing and Midwifery in Canada*. (2010). Myra Rutherdale (Ed.). McGill-Queen's University Press.

*Caring and Curing. Health and Medicine in Western Religious Tradition*. (1986). Ronald L. Numbers and Darrel W. Amundsen (Eds.). Macmillan.

*Catholic Witness to Healthcare. Practicing Medicine in Truth and Love*. (2017). John M. Travaline, John M. Mitchell and Louise A. Mitchell (Eds). The Catholic University of America Press.

Crislip, Andrew T. (2005). *From Monastery to Hospital. Christian Monasticism and the Transformation of Health Care in Late Antiquity*. University of Michigan Press.

Curtis, Heather D. (2007). *Faith in the Great Physician. Suffering and Divine Healing in American Culture. 1860–1900*. Johns Hopkins University Press.

Dossey, Barbara M. (2010). Florence Nightingale. A 19th Century Mystic. *Journal of Holistic Nursing*, 28 (1), 10–35.

Ferngren, Gary B. (2009). *Medicine and Health Care in Early Christianity*. Johns Hopkins University Press.

Fox, Bethany McKinney. (2019). *Disability and the Way of Jesus. Holistic Healing in the Gospels and the Church*. Downers IVP Academic.

Harris, Ruth. (1999). *Lourdes. Body and Spirit in the Secular Age*. Penguin Books.

Klassen, Pamela E. (2011). *Spirits of Protestantism: Medicine, Healing, and Liberal Christianity*. University of California Press.

Maher, P. (2006). Reclaiming Spirituality in Nursing. *A History of Nursing Ideas*. L. Andrist, P. Nicolas, and K. Wolf (Eds.). Jones and Bartlett Company.

McCrary, Lorraine Krall. (2017). Geel's Family Care Tradition: Care, Communities, and the Social Inclusion of Persons with Disabilities. *Journal of Literacy and Cultural Disability Studies*, 11 (3), 285–301.

Morelli, George. (2006). *Healing, Orthodox Christianity and Scientific Psychology*. Eastern Church Publishing.

Nurriddin, Ayah, Graham Mooney, and Alexandre White. (2020). Reckoning with Histories of Medical Racism and Violence in the USA. *The Lancet* (British Edition 396), 949–51.

*Nursing in Society. A Historical Perspective*. Fifteenth Edition. (1983). Josephine A. Dolan, M. Louise Fitzpatrick, and Eleanor Krohn Herrmann (Eds.). W.B. Saunders Company.

O'Brien, Mary-Elizabeth. (2022). *Spirituality in Nursing. Standing on Holy Ground*. Seventh Edition. Jone & Bartlett Learning.

O'Brien, Mary-Elizabeth. (2010). *Servant Leadership: Spirituality and Practice in Contemporary Health Care*. Jones and Bartlett.

O'Brien, Mary-Elizabeth. (2008). *A Sacred Covenant. The Spiritual Ministry of Nursing*. Jones and Bartlett.

Opp, James. (2005). *The Lord For the Body. Religion, Medicine and Protestant Faith Healing 1880–1930*. McGill-Queens.

Porterfield, Amanda. (2005). *Healing in the History of Christianity*. Oxford University Press.

Remus, Harold. (1997). *Jesus as Healer*. Cambridge University Press.

Roosens, Eugeen and Lieve Van de Walle. (2007). *Geel Revisited. After Centuries of Mental Rehabilitation*. Garant.

Scribner, Susan et al. (2020). Bridges to Care and Recovery. Addressing Behavioral and Mental Health Needs Through the Faith Community. *Journal of Religion and Health*, 59 (4), 1946–57.

Stahl, Devan. (2020). Reimagining the Healing Service. *Theology Today*, 77 (2), 165–78.

Stanley, Ruth. (December 2009). Types of Prayer, Heart Rate Variability and Innate Healing. *Zygon: Journal of Religion and Science*, 44 (4), 825–46.

Stevis-Gridneff, Matina and Kobe Ryckewaert. (2023). A Radical Experiment in Mental Health Care Tested Over Centuries. *The New York Times*, April 21, 2023.

Wainwright, Elaine. (2017). *Women Healing/Healing Women: The Genderization Of Healing in Early Christianity*. Taylor and Francis.

Wilson, Walter T. (2014). *Healing in the Gospel of Matthew. Reflections on Method and Ministry*. Fortress Press.

Broadway Housing Communities: https://www.broadwayhousing.org/

https://www.npr.org/sections/health-shots/2016/07/01/484083305/for-centuries-a-small-town-has-embraced-strangers-with-mental-illness

## CITY OF MIRACLES

https://www.youtube.com/watch?v=56LPgXO7PXM

Principles of Integrative Nursing, Earl E. Bakken Center for Spirituality and Healing: https://csh.umn.edu/academics/focus-areas/integrative-nursing/principles-integrative-nursing

# 10 Allah Shall Heal the Hearts of All Believers: Islam and Healing

The Muslim tradition is based upon the teachings and life example of the Prophet Muhammad who lived in the 7th century CE in what is now Saudi Arabia. According to Muslim tradition the angel Jibril (Gabriel) dictated the Qur'an to the prophet Muhammad between 610 and 632 CE. Islam is a monotheistic religion with an emphasis on ethical action in the world embodied in a law code called the *shari'ah*.

While Muslims revere prophets such as Noah and Moses, and the Qur'an includes Jesus (Isa) and the Virgin Mary, Muhammad is considered to be the final prophet. His teachings and actions recorded by his followers in the *hadith*, are considered to be the primary guides for a Muslim life.

Muslims believe in Allah—the one God whose will is expressed through his angels, prophets and scripture. The unity of God (*tawhid*) is a foundational part of Muslim theology. The tradition also emphasizes the equality of all before God and the world-wide community of Islam (*ummah*).

The Five Pillars of Islam are the obligatory practice of all Muslims which are: *shahadah*, the profession of faith, *salat* (prayers) five times a day at dawn, noon, mid-afternoon, sunset, and after dark, *zakat* alms given for care of those in need, *sawm* (fasting), the annual month long fast of Ramadan, and *hajj*, the pilgrimage to Mecca. Over time the Muslim tradition developed streams of Sunni and Shi'ism, and the mystical branch of Sufism.

DOI: 10.4324/9781003471769-10

Islam spread rapidly from it base in Arabia across Central Asia and North Africa, South and Southeast Asia, and as far as Spain. This culture referred to as Dar al-Islam was a system of trade, politics, religion, and culture. Islam coming into contact with many different cultures created complex religious and medical cultures. In the contemporary period large Muslim communities can be found throughout the world.

Conceptions of health and healing within the Muslim tradition are understood within the larger framework of the *tawhid* (unity, oneness) of Allah. Any understanding of health is based in the belief that God is all powerful and sovereign and so all healing is believed to be coming from the divine. In the Qur'an Allah is referred by the epithet Al-Shafi—the Restorer of Health (41: 44). This power of granting health and healing can be mediated in a variety of ways including through doctors, healers, lifestyle, medicine, and prayer.

While depicting the divine is not permitted in the Muslim tradition, the attributes of Allah can be gleaned from the traditional 99 names. These include Allah described as Al-Shafi (the Healer), Al-Raham (the Compassionate), and Al-Rahim (The Merciful). From within this worldview the divine oversees all aspects of life and well-being and with the "best of all remedies according to the Hadith is the Qur'an" (Doumato, 2000, p. 134). From a Muslim point of view health is a great blessing second only to having faith. The Qur'an is viewed as being fundamentally healing in itself and states, "We send down the Qu'ran as healing and mercy to those who believe" (p. 82).

Continual remembrance of God, giving to charity, fasting, ethical action, and following the commandments of the tradition are all considered to contribute to both physical and psychological well-being. The primary modes of remembrance are *salat* (prayer), both the five cycles of obligatory prayer each day, and *dhikr* (recitation).

As Rahman (1988) has argued, "Islam, as a religion has played a fundamental role in the creation of a culture that has nurtured the cultivation and development of medicine" (p. 149). This culture has been concretized in Muslim civilizations and communities in a variety of ways that include the building of hospitals by the 8th century CE in Damascus and Baghdad. and the development of a variety of forms of healing.

The Prophet Muhammad is the paradigmatic figure of the tradition and his teachings and actions are the model of life for all Muslims. The records of his actions in the *sunnah* and *hadith* offer the model accepted by the community. Healing practices based on the actions of the Prophet, his Companions, and Holy Men and Women are called *Tibb an-Nabawi* (Medicine of the Prophet). The prophet Muhammad is understood as being part of the lineage of the holy figures such as Zakariah and Isa (Jesus) who were noted for the powers of healing. Accounts are given in the scripture of the Prophet Muhammad healing his followers.

In the recorded accounts of his life the Prophet Muhammad is described as seeking out both religious and naturalistic approaches to healing. As a result, it is considered obligatory for Muslims to access medical care when necessary. The hadith states that "The Prophet said, 'There is no disease that Allah has created, except that He also has created its treatment'" (Sahih al Bukhari 5678).

The Qur'an and sunnah recognize the need for protection against various malevolent forces which can contribute to bad fortune and ill health. In these cases, only Prophetic Medicine is deemed to be efficacious. As the Islamic world is vast and takes in many cultures some practices are influenced by regional traditions. Practices of using sections of scripture placed within amulets remain typical in the Middle East and Mediterranean world.

Understandings of the causes of illness in Islam are complex. Some conditions are viewed as purely the result of physical conditions but others are seen as serving a religious function. These can include the idea that they may be purifying, a punishment for sin, or a trial leading to long-term blessings.

Regardless of the reasons for an illness, the ethical prescription of mercy ensures that the first reaction is always to show compassion for those who are suffering. The *hadith* emphasizes the merit that is accrued by visiting the sick. Detailed instruction is given regarding keeping visits short so as not to tire the person and to try to buoy their spirits and encourage them. It is also understood that the patient is in a state of purity and therefore closer to the divine and can pray effectively for others.

Use of prayer and recitation is a central part of Muslim healing practices. The hadith places a particular emphasis on communal prayer which is viewed as more effective. The practice of *dua* (supplication) and *ruqyah* use the recitation of *surahs* (chapters) from the Qur'an. The first chapter and final chapters being deemed especially powerful in relation to healing. These practices are ideally to be performed after ensuring cleanliness of one's body and clothes and have particular efficacy if done at auspicious times and in holy places such Mecca and Jerusalem.

*Allahuma rabbi-nas adhhabal ba'sa, ashfi wa entashafi, la shifa' illa shifa'uka shifa' la yughadiru saqama.*

Oh Allah! The Sustainer of Mankind! Remove the illness, cure the disease. You are the One Who cures. There is no cure except Your cure. Grant us a cure that leaves no illness. (Recommended to touch the area of pain with the right hand while reciting this supplication.)

'As'alu Allah al 'azim rabbil 'arshil azim an yashifika.

I ask Allah, the Mighty, the Lord of the Mighty Throne, to cure you. (Recommended to repeat seven times.)

A'oozu bi'izzatillaahi wa qudratihi min sharri maa ajidu wa uhaaziru.

I seek protection in the might of Allah and His power from the evil of what I am experiencing and of what I fear. (Recommended for the sick person to place right hand on area of pain, say Bismillah three times, then recite this supplication seven times.)

—Children's National Hospital, Chaplaincy Services

## ISLAM AND SOCIAL WELFARE

Any understanding of health and well-being in the Muslim tradition has to include ideals of social welfare. The *zakhat* the fourth pillar of Islam is a tithe that traditionally went towards the larger community and the care of the widow, orphan, and others in need. Belief in the responsibility of community towards each other creates an overarching framework that calls for physical, mental, and spiritual care. This also emphasizes a holistic view of health and healing that includes belief in the sanctity of life and the call to alleviate suffering. Islamic law also addresses itself to lifestyle and behaviour that promotes health emphasizing hygiene, and forbidding the consumption of alcohol and pork.

A contributing stream to this support of the social welfare is the idea of the Islamic *ummah* and mutual responsibility within the community. This has been expressed in the teaching of the diseased limb. This concept establishes the belief that if one part of the community is suffering then it impacts the whole. In this organic metaphor of community as body, any sickness must be healed for the good of the whole.

The emphasis on unity and mutual obligation within the *ummah* is illustrated in the hadith on Brotherhood.

> Al-Nu'man ibn Bashir reported: The Messenger of Allah, peace and blessings be upon him, said, "The parable of the believers in their affection, mercy, and compassion for each other is that of a body. When any limb aches, the whole body reacts with sleeplessness and fever".
>
> (*Ṣaḥīḥ al-Bukhārī6011, Ṣaḥīḥ Muslim 2586*)

This idea is invoked in calls for intervention in cases where aid is required such as the case of taking care of refugees. This emphasis on group welfare has also resulted in the creation of international bodies such as the Red Crescent Society, a humanitarian organization created to send aid in times of war or other emergencies.

Islamic rulers founded libraries in cities such as Cairo, Aleppo, and across Central Asia and into what is now Spain. These became repositories of medical knowledge from Egyptian, Greek, Persian, and Roman culture and also served to spur on new medical discoveries.

The interest of the early caliphs in medicine resulted in the creation of bureaus in Baghdad set up to translate Greek, Indian, and Persian works into Arabic. This enormous project included the work of Muslim, Jewish, and Christian translators and doctors.

In the earliest political forms created within Islam under the first Caliphates health and healing were part of the political mandate of these leaders. Residences were built for lepers and the blind by the Umayyad caliph al-Walid. Medical treatment was offered free of charge and was often open to non-Muslims and also often extended to the animal world.

The first hospitals in the Islamic world were founded in Damascus and Baghdad in the early 10th century The caliphs sponsored a variety of healing institutions. such as the Mansuri Hospital built in Cairo in 1283. The hospital included a wing for the mentally ill and the larger complex featured a mosque for Muslims and a chapel for Christians. The expressed intent was for the institution to serve all, "men and women, rich or poor who live in Cairo and its surroundings" (Isa Bib 1939: 138).

## THE PHYSICIAN IN MUSLIM CULTURE

Muslim physicians functioned within the pluralistic world of the medieval period and were in close contact with Christian, Jewish, and Indian practitioners. Drawing on the Hippocratic Corpus and the work of Galen it was also common for Muslim doctors to take the Hippocratic oath. The role of the doctor was considered to be a calling and not to be undertaken purely for material gain.

One of the paradigmatic examples of the physician is al-Rāzī, (Rhazes), born *c.* 854. Both Muslim philosopher and doctor al-Razi is often considered one of the greatest physicians of the Islamic world. This mixture of scholar/physician was typical of Muslim approaches to the practice of medicine. Health and healing were "based in religion and culture, obeying codes of ethics" and also being responsive to the relationships with patients, colleagues, and the larger community (Falagas et al., 2006, p. 1583).

Like many intellectuals of the time al-Razi worked at various royal courts. He viewed himself as the Islamic version of Socratic philosopher and inheritor of the mantle of Hippocrates. Al-Rāzī's two most significant medical works are the *Kitāb al-Manṣūrī*, and *Kitab-al bawi*, the Comprehensive Book. In these works, he surveyed Greek, Syrian, and early Arabic medicine as well as some Indian medical knowledge. Throughout his works he recorded his own judgement and medical experiences with patients as commentary.

Another pre-eminent figure in the Islamic world was Ibn Sina (Avicenna) (*c.* 970–1037) who led a peripatetic life in the turbulent political world of the time. In his work he combined the disparate strands Greek late antiquity and early Islam into a system that encompassed and harmonized revelation and rationalistic discourse.

Among his numerous works were the influential *Treatise on the Small Pox and Measles*, which was translated into Latin, Greek, and various modern languages. Ibn Sina completed his major work, *The Cure* (*al-Shifā'*) while living in the court of Ala'ad-Dawla in Isfahan in what is now Iran.

Both al-Razi and Ibn Sina represent the medieval Muslim ideal of the physician/philosopher. Various Muslims states vied for the services of scholars and this led to what has been referred to as the Golden Age of Arabic Science (8th to 13th century CE). One of the most celebrated examples is found in Al-Andalus, Islamic Spain, where intellectuals of various backgrounds gathered to share in their discoveries. Within these courts intellectuals, philosophers, and doctors of Muslim, Jewish, and Christian backgrounds were able to practice freely.

## THE UNANI TRADITION AND THE ROLE OF THE HAKIM

The Unani system developed from the Graeco-Arabic work of Avicenna, Hippocrates, and Galen. By the 13th century CE Unani medicine was spread throughout the Muslim world (Dar al-Islam) which included the Indian sub-continent. In India, over the centuries, it developed its own distinct medical culture interacting with Indian systems such as Ayurveda.

Mughal emperors, such as Babur, supported the writing of medical texts and their courts attracted physicians from Central Asia and Iran. Within this context Muslim hakims and Hindu vaids worked together in compiling pharmacopeia and working in hospitals. Patronage of medicine was a central part of the Mughal form of governance.

The first hakims wrote in Persian and were examples of a sophisticated cosmopolitan culture, "in tune with the historical, literary, and medical cultures of the world" (Alavi, 2008, p. 35). Typically, they wrote encyclopaedias which were a compendium of knowledge drawn from Graeco-Arabic and Indian culture. While including lists of drugs and practices, health for the early hakim included being a cultured person emphasizing proper comportment and etiquette.

With the decline of Mughal power in the 18th century the Unani system increasingly came into contact with European approaches to medicine. The British colonial power hired both Muslim and Hindu doctors to work as public servants particularly in the army. This resulted in a hybrid system and many hakims worked in vaccination campaigns and at dispensaries.

With the political changes that resulted in India gaining its independence, the Indian government established official recognition of Unani medicine. The Indian Medicine Central Council (IMCC) Act was implemented in 1970 and regulates education and practice in the Unani system of medicine with their own institutions of research and training. In Pakistan hakims are an integral part of the medical landscape. Currently hakims practice in India, Pakistan, and Bangladesh maintaining a holistic approach to health including attention to diet and lifestyle.

## HEALING IN THE SUFI TRADITION

Sufism, the mystical branch of Islam, retains an enduring connection with healing and Sufis are commonly associated with healing miracles. After their death the graves of Sufi Pirs (saints) became sites of pilgrimage where visitors would seek various interventions with the divine including for health. These tomb/shrines exist across the Muslim world from North Africa to South Asia.

Sites such as the Nizamuddin Auliya *dargah* (shrine) in New Delhi, India have been renowned as spiritual and healing centres. Devotional music is performed daily by qawwali singers for visitors who come from a variety of religious backgrounds. The *dargah* has been referred to as a "a spiritual hub in Delhi's heart" by the *Times of India*.

Sufi healers are also ubiquitous across the Muslim world. In Joyce Burkhalter Flueckiger's (2006) ethnography of a healer based in Hyderabad, India she demonstrates the web of relationships that uphold the authority of the healer. The efficacy of the prescriptions given are seen as being based in her spiritual discipline, intention, and connection to Sufi lineages.

These healers typically offer their services to all regardless of religious background. The epithet Amma, meaning mother, is common to female healers and gurus in India. However her practices are demarcated as Muslim by the emphasis on the written word and being situated within the context of Sunni and Shi'I religious symbolism.

The healer is also clear about the parameters of her healing ability, often suggesting the person consult a physician if the problem lays outside her scope of power. Amma also directs her clients to various herbalists in the community. Diagnosis is achieved by a variety of methods including forms of mathematics and palm reading. Amma specializes in problems related to evil forces brought on by malevolent beings or the evil eye (*nazar*).

The Sufi tradition also developed the idea of the non-physical body the *nasma* which is influenced and moved into imbalance and illness by improper diet and conduct. From this view of the subtle aspects of health and healing, "In the health system, the energies in each body not only remain balanced but also support and influence the energy balance in other peoples' bodies" (Kabbani, 2013, p. 51). Sufi healers are understood as receiving certain gifts, including the gift of healing, as a result of their spiritual discipline and devotion.

## Dr Inez Jinnah

### Family and Palliative Care Physician

### How would you say Islam influences you in your work?

It infuses everything that I do. It comes through in how I speak with my patients and in my care for them. I was taught by my father, who was also a physician, that it is very important to treat people the way that you would want to be treated. When talking to someone imagine yourself in their position.

### Do you feel that this can get lost in the current system of health care?

Well, especially now when our system is under stress and people are very busy it can be necessary to make a conscious effort to remember this is not just a patient but also a person.

### Do you feel that the practice of medicine is a vocation/calling?

People go into medicine for a variety of reasons, and all have to work very hard. But there is always the element of compassion. The Qur'an does teach that you should help wherever you can. The gifts given to you should be used to help others. I was provided the opportunity, the finances and the time, to fulfill this role so I should use it for the good of my family, my community and my society. Islam teaches us to spend of what we have, including money, time, knowledge to benefit all around us.

### How do you think that religion can function best in a secular society?

I don't see the dichotomy. In Canada we have the privilege to practice our profession in a way that doesn't conflict with religion. I am legally obligated to provide my patients with all their available options.

## Does having religious faith help you to stay centred in challenging situations?

As I Muslim I am comforted by knowing that God's will decides everything. Things happen and they happen for a reason. We are asked by God to always show mercy and to alleviate suffering wherever possible. Muslims believe in the afterlife and that this life is one part of a much longer story.

It is my role to offer assistance and to help my patients navigate and to be a reliable source of assistance. So, I give my phone number and they can call anytime. No one has ever abused that system. I am available for them.

That said I know many people who are not religious who for instance visit people when they are sick. I have a patient who is 87 who visits people regularly and volunteers—he just does it because he feels it is the right thing to do.

## How did you become interested in palliative care?

I became interested over 25 years ago. It was through Dr Brian Shaw, he taught me how to talk to patients, the right approach. And then I was asked to join a palliative care committee. In palliative care I am privileged to be there for people at a very emotional time and to provide assistance. We provided excellent care within the hospital and now have a hospice.

## In the early days of palliative care there was a lot of controversy around whether or not the physician should tell a patient their condition was terminal. What are your thoughts on this?

I find this is very cultural. I had a case in the ICU where the daughter-in-law did not want me to tell the patient. But things are changing we now have Advance Directives to guide us. We also have the SPIKES protocol (a six-step protocol for breaking bad news).

## Is there a Muslim idea of a "good death"?

Not specifically because again the time of death is part of the will of God. Islam teaches that you should remember your death every day, not in a morbid way but in order to maintain a larger perspective.

But there is a general idea that the person should be at peace with themselves, comfortable, and surrounded by family. But the central idea is that if you are at peace with life and what you have done, it doesn't really matter where you are.

## OVERVIEW OF ISLAM

Founder: The Prophet Muhammad (570–632 CE).

Estimated Number of Followers: 1 billion.

Largest Muslim populations are found in Indonesia, Pakistan, India, Bangladesh with significant populations in Canada, the US, the UK, France, and Germany.

Main Divisions: Sunni, Shi'i, Ismaili.

Scripture: The Qur'an.

Other important writings: Hadith (sayings of the Prophet), sunnah (habitual practices).

Core Beliefs: The tawhid (unity of God); Five Pillars of Islam: Shahadat, Salat (obligatory prayers five times a day), Ramadan, Zakat (charitable giving), and Pilgrimage (hajj); Beliefs Regarding the Afterlife: Final Judgement and belief in Heaven and Hell.

Religious Specialists: In the Sunni tradition the imam leads the community prayers and often oversees the mosque/masjid.

Muslims practice burial ideally within 24 hours of death. Traditionally members of the community wash and prepare the body for burial in a white cotton garment.

The Shahadah (Muslim Profession of Faith).

There is no god but Allah and Muhammad is the messenger of God.

## REFERENCES

Allah Shall Heal the Hearts of All Believers Surah Al-Tawba: 14

Alavi, Seema. (2008). *Islam and Healing. Loss and Recovery of An Indo Muslim Medical tradition, 1600–1900*. Palgrave Macmillan.

Doumato, Eleanor Abdella. (2000). *Getting God's Ear. Women, Islam and Healing in Saudi Arabia and the Gulf*. Columbia University Press.

Falagas, Matthew E., Effie A. Zarkadoulis, and George Samonis. (August, 2006). Arab Science in the Golden Age (750–1258 CE) and Today. *FASEB Journal*, 20 (10), 1581–6.

Flueckiger, Joyce Burkhalter. (2006). *In Amma's Healing Room. Gender And Vernacular Islam in South India*. Indiana University Press.

Isa Bib, Ahmad. (1939). *Tarikh al-Bimaristani fi'l-Islam* (History of hospitals in Islam). al-Matba'a al-Hashimiya.

Kabbani, Shaykh Muhammad Hisham. (2013). *The Principles of Islamic Spirituality. Part One: Sufism*. Islamic Supreme Council of America.

Rahman, Fazlur. (1988). *Health and Medicine in the Islamic Tradition*. Crossroads Publishing Company.

Shaykh Muhammad Hisham Kabbani. (2013). *Principles of Islamic Spirituality. Part Two. Contemporary Sufism and Traditional Islamic Healing*. Institute for Spiritual and Cultural Advancement.

## FURTHER READING

Abu-Zahra, Nadia. (2000). *The Pure and the Powerful. Studies in Contemporary Muslim Society*. Ithaca Press.

Al-Razi, Abu Bakr. (1950). *The Spiritual Physick of Rhazes*. Arthur J. Arberry. (Trans.). Paragon Book Gallery Ltd.

Al. Shahabi, Shams Ul Din. (1996). *Al-Tibb An-Nawawi* (*Medicine of the Prophet*). Maktabar Nizar Mustafa al Baz.

Bynum, William. (2008). *The History of Medicine. A Very Short Introduction*. Oxford University Press.

Dols, Michael. (1985). *Medieval Islamic Medicine*. University of California Press.

Gohlman, W. E. (1974). *The Life of Ibn Sina*. SUNY Press.

Hussein, Rassoul G. (December 2000). The Crescent and Islam: Healing, Nursing and the Spiritual Dimensions. Some considerations Towards an Understanding of the Islamic Perspectives on Caring. *Journal of Advanced Nursing*, 32 (6), 1476–84.

*Islam, Sufism and the Everyday Politics of Belonging in South Asia*. (2016). Deepra Dandekar and Torsten Tschacher (Eds.). Routledge.

Jankowsky, Richard C. (2021). *Ambient Sufism. Ritual Niches and the Social Work of Musical Form*. The University of Chicago Press.

Khan, Muhammad Salim. (1986). *Islamic Medicine*. Routledge.

Mitha, Karim. (July–September, 2019). Sufism and Healing. *Journal of Spirituality in Mental Health*, 21 (3),194–205.

Mushtaq and Margoob. "Pir, Faqr and Psychotherapist."

Nizamuddin Dargah: A Spiritual Hub in the Heart of the (*sic*) Delhi, *Times of India*, October 25, 2023.

Shaikh, Babar T. and Juanita Hatcher. (2005). Complementary and Alternative Medicine in Pakistan: Prospects and Limitations. *Evidence Based Complementary and Alternative Medicine*. 2 (2), 139–42.

Yucel, Salih. (2010). *Prayer and Healing in Islam*. Tughra Books.

# 11 Subtle Bodies: Metaphysical Traditions of Healing

For anyone living in a town or city in North America a wide array of "alternative" health practitioners are often readily available. These can include chiropractors, osteopaths, practitioners of Reiki and Therapeutic Touch, Naturopaths, Iridologists, Homeopaths, and Reflexologists. These modalities emerged from various spiritual influences and all share a holistic vision of human health that takes in both mental and spiritual aspects of health and healing.

Many of these forms of healing derive from esoteric, occult, and New Religious movements. Because these metaphysical beliefs and techniques aren't necessarily affiliated with specific religious denominations, practitioners often combine ideas from a variety of sources. Techniques can include: body work, energy healing, meditation, visualization, and affirmation among many other approaches.

Many metaphysical healing practices developed from the harmonial traditions of North America. This approach downplayed religious denominations and divisions and shares an optimistic, eclectic approach to both spirituality and healing. The counterculture of the 1960s was the engine behind the acceptance of many of these practices such as body work and practices of divination and astrology came into the mainstream.

Alongside the "turn East" and an interest in the practice of Hinduism and Buddhism was an interest in diets including macrobiotic, vegetarianism, and veganism. These have since come increasingly into the mainstream with healthcare workers such as chiropractors, osteopaths, and Reiki practitioners once referred as "quacks" rapidly becoming an accepted part of the healthcare landscape.

DOI: 10.4324/9781003471769-11

The spiritual basis of these approaches varies as many practitioners are explicitly religious while others would understand themselves as being spiritual and drawing from a variety of traditions. This is true both of the healers and those who seek their services. This less boundaried sense of spirituality emerged in what came to be called the New Age Movement in the late 1970s and 1980s.

This stream of spirituality speaks to the rise of the religious "nones"- those who have no religious affiliation. Close to a quarter of all people in North America now identify as having no affiliation with a religious tradition. This does not necessarily mean, however, that they are atheists and many identify as "spiritual but not religious".

Metaphysical healers also reject the machine model of the human body. Drawing on Hindu, Buddhist, Chinese, and occult sources they generally view the body as a system of energy. Many have developed their own version of the chakra system found within tantric Hinduism and work with energy is generally a part of healing. The body is understood as being an aspect of consciousness and possessing its own wisdom. Most emphasize the divinity of the body and use a variety of methods including massage, touch, sound, and crystals to work with its energy.

Metaphysical approaches to healing are also often closely aligned and practiced alongside various forms of psychology. The emphasis on the mind and mental states is central to the idea developed by New Thought. This stream of thought emphasized the divinity within and the ability to heal all aspects of one's life leading to a state of physical, mental, and economic well-being.

The central role of women in these movements is an important part of their development. Often barred from participation in leadership roles in mainstream religions, and in medicine, by the 19th century women were instrumental in the rise of New Religious Movements (NRMs). Many of these movements were politically radical questioning traditional ideas about gender and power. It is unsurprising, then, that they also supported countercultural approaches to health and healing just as physicalist medicine was approaching its zenith of power and prestige.

## "LIFE IN AND OF THE SPIRIT": CHRISTIAN SCIENCE AND HEALTH

One of the most influential of the metaphysical healing movements was Christian Science, Church of Christ Scientist. The broad outlines of the life and work of founder Mary Baker Eddy (1821–1910) became a kind of template for the New Age healers who followed. Eddy developed a sophisticated and centrally organized religious and healing movement that gained followers throughout North America and internationally.

Eddy was born on a farm in New Hampshire and much of her childhood and adult life was spent in ill health. As result she became immersed in the what Albanese (2007) calls "the spiritual seeker culture of her age" (p. 284). This was a period of profound change in American history. Many New Religious Movements such as the Church of the Latter-Day Saints, Spiritualism, the Shakers, and various Utopian communities developed in the region of Upstate New York.

These movements were responding to the growing challenges to more traditional religion and the upheaval caused by the Industrial Revolution. Part of this burgeoning milieu, Eddy became a patient of the healer Phineas Parkhurst Quimby, whose medicine-free healing techniques influenced her greatly. When she first visited Quimby in 1862 she was a virtual invalid and with his help her health quickly improved. Mary Baker Eddy understood this as an illustration of the words of Jesus, "Thy faith hath made thee whole".

A few weeks after Quimby's death in 1866, Eddy injured her back and neck. She came to see this incident as the turning point in her life and the beginning of a sense of mission. According to this narrative it was reading about one of the healing miracles of Jesus that triggered Eddy's full recovery and discovery of Christian Science. The stated aim, according to Eddy (1899) was "to reinstate primitive Christianity and its lost element of healing" (p. 3).

At the core of Christian Science is the teaching that God and God's creation are entirely good and spiritual and that God has made all things in his likeness. Christian Scientists see this spiritual perspective as the only reality and all else as illusion or error. Christian Science is the most idealist of the metaphysical approaches. This radical optimism came to characterize much of New Age thinking. Prayer, from the Christian Science perspective, does not ask God to intervene, but is a process of awakening to spiritual truth.

Some Christian Scientists rejected the use of biomedical doctors or the use of drugs or surgery while others use both the service of biomedicine and prayer. Healing was to occur as a result of a Christian Science treatment, a specific form of prayer intended to spiritualize thought. Part of the job of the healer from this perspective was to recognize that the person was already well if they could break through misperception.

For those who practice Christian Science prayer is a vital tool in the spiritualization of thought and a way to gain an understanding of God. Prayer is believed to heal the distortion, bringing spiritual reality which is equated with the Kingdom of Heaven described by Jesus. From this point of view faith is a vital part of healing. According to Eddy, in order to practice Christian Science effectively one must practice prayer and undertake the moral regeneration of one's life. She was quick to point that the healings weren't meant to be an end in themselves but rather that they attest to the truth of a Higher Reality.

Christian Scientists continue to run institutions and to sponsor healers, reading rooms and the publication *The Christian Science Monitor* founded in 1908 by Mary Baker Eddy. The larger Christian Science movement has been credited with inspiring a renewed focus on healing within mainstream Christian communities.

> On the third day thereafter, I called for my Bible, and opened it at Matthew ix. 2. As I read, the healing Truth dawned upon my sense; and the result was that I rose, dressed myself, and ever after was in better health than I had before enjoyed. That short experience included a glimpse and of Spirit; this Life being the sole reality of existence.
>
> (Eddy, 1900, Miscellaneous Writings, 24, pp. 1–18)

## VANGUARD OF THE NEW AGE: THEOSOPHY AND THERAPEUTIC TOUCH

From its founding in New York City in 1875 Theosophy attracted those who were open and interested in alternative forms of healing. Helena Blavatsky, Theosophy's main ideologue, is now often referred to as "Mother of the New Age Movement". The Theosophical society was the group most responsible for introducing concepts such as karma, reincarnation, and as the idea of chakras into the western world. They were also part of the revival of interest in astrology.

In order to create a philosophy that could address a variety of new challenges the Theosophists drew upon religious and philosophical concepts derived from both eastern and western sources. Theosophists tended to be politically radical and open to alternative forms of politics, economics, and healing. While biomedicine was moving into an ascendant position in the field of health many Theosophists championed alternative, more spiritually based forms of healing, which included various forms of energy healing. The open theology of the Theosophical movement attracted many who were interested in a variety of approaches to heath including: osteopaths, massage therapists and energy healers, iridologists, homeopaths, and diets such as vegetarianism.

## DORA KUNZ, DELORES KRIEGER, AND THE DEVELOPMENT OF THERAPEUTIC TOUCH

The most influential approach to healing to emerge directly from Theosophy was Therapeutic Touch developed by Dora Kunz and Delores Kreiger. Kunz was born into a Theosophical family in 1904 during the period of Dutch colonization of Java. As a child she was taught meditation and exposed to a wide variety of religions. As an adult Kunz moved to the United States and began work as a clairvoyant with a particular interest in medical intuition.

According to Kunz, Therapeutic Touch (TT) was an ancient technique, such as the Christian laying on of hands, practiced across the world's religions. However, in developing her technique she opened the practice out to all backgrounds, including those who did not consider themselves to be religious. Kunz and Krieger emphasized that spontaneous cures were not the aim of Therapeutic Touch rather it was meant to bring order to disordered energy and support the natural healing process of the mind and body.

Therapeutic Touch views the body as an open energy system that can become disordered. This disorder, then, and lead to illness. From this perspective the energy system of the human body can be impacted by the energy of others. There is an emphasis on calming and centring that can be used by both the practitioner and the person receiving the treatment.

In the 1960s Kunz began working with doctors and nurses noting that she preferred this as they were accustomed to dealing with those who were in pain. Over time the technique was taught to anyone who wished to heal others. Kunz worked closely with Otellia Bengston, allergist and immunologist and Robert Laidlaw, Chief of Psychiatry at the Roosevelt Hospital in New York and in 1975 an accredited course was developed by New York University. Therapeutic

Touch is now an accepted part of training for nurses and practiced in hospitals and health agencies around the globe.

A person's aura is their emotional energy manifesting around—actually interpenetrating—the body. Sending goodwill and energy for the healing of a disease positively affects the aura of both therapist and patient. This is basic to the Therapeutic Touch process. The moment a person gets upset, those feelings are at once distributed in the aura. If the energy is intense it affects the chakras. A Therapeutic Touch treatment changes the color and subtle energy patterns of the patient's aura as the patient lessens and then loses his anxiety.

(Kunz and Krieger, 2004, p. 151)

## LOUISE HAY: QUEEN OF THE NEW AGE

Louise Hay (1926–2017) bridges the ideas developed within New Thought and Christian Science into the New Age. Hay, moved through a number of careers before becoming a spiritual leader and founding Hay House, a publishing house dedicated to self-help and inspirational writing. Hay embodied in her own life and teaching the eclectic beliefs and optimism of the New Age movement.

Undoubtedly one of the reasons for Hay's popularity was her embodiment of the archetype of the wounded healer as someone who had overcome personal adversity. According to her account she had an extremely traumatic childhood in an impoverished family and was the victim of both physical and sexual abuse.

After leaving home and struggling financially, she managed to create a life for herself working as a model and eventually marrying. However, in middle age she was divorced and then faced a health crisis. Hay viewed this period in her life as a watershed and at this time she found the First Church of Religious Science, in New York City.

Hay began to study the New Thought works of authors like Florence Scovel Shinn, who claimed that positive thinking could change people's material circumstances, and the Religious Science founder Ernest Holmes who taught that positive thinking could heal the body. Hay also studied Transcendental Meditation. In the early 1970s she became a Religious Science practitioner and popular workshop leader. In this role she led people in spoken affirmations which she believed led to physical, mental, and emotional well-being.

Hay writes that in the late 1970s she was diagnosed with incurable cervical cancer. Based on her training she he came to the conclusion that by holding on to resentment for her childhood abuse and rape she had contributed to its onset of the disease in that part of her body. Hay (1984) believed that "The body, like everything else in life, is a mirror of our inner thoughts and beliefs. The body is always talking to us if we will only listen" (p. 123).

She decided to try to heal herself and refused conventional medical treatment for six months, and began a regime of forgiveness, coupled with therapy, nutrition, reflexology, and enemas. This story was based on her testimony and was not confirmed by a doctor in any of the written material.

Around the same time as her recovery she began leading support groups for people living with HIV or AIDS. These grew from a few people in her living room to hundreds of men in a large hall in West Hollywood. Through her work with AIDS, she became well known and was invited to appear on television becoming one of the first New Age celebrities.

In 1984, Hay's book *You Can Heal Your Life* landed on the *New York Times* best-seller list. More than 50 million copies have now been sold around the world in over 30 languages. Hay connected various illnesses to specific thought patterns and emphasized the power of affirmations that could be repeated aloud daily. These practices along with healthy diet and attitudes of gratitude and forgiveness were presented as key to healing. Contemporary research has borne out many of Hay's teaching regarding the connection between attitudes and the body and her techniques are widely used by healers and psychologists.

## *Affirmation*

In the infinity of life where I am,
all is perfect, whole, and complete.
I believe in a power far greater than I am
that flows through me every moment of every day.
I open myself to the wisdom within,
knowing there is only One Intelligence in this Universe.
Out of this One Intelligence comes all the answers,
all the solutions, all the healings, all the new creations.

I trust this Power and Intelligence,
knowing that whatever I need to know is revealed to me,
and that whatever I need comes to me
in the right time, space, and sequence.
All is well in my world.

(Hay, 1984, p. 9)

## OVERVIEW OF METAPHYSICAL TRADITIONS

Metaphysical ideas are eclectic and varied by their nature. Typically, they embody an optimistic view of human nature and focus on development and self-actualization and improvement.

A person may practice metaphysical approaches while being a member of a religion or having no set religious beliefs.

These approaches are typically holistic emphasizing mind, body, and soul and understand the body as an energy system.

Often include psychologically inflected approaches to healing.

Those interested in metaphysical approaches often take the "turn East" and are interested in concepts derived from world religions such as Hinduism and Buddhism.

## REFERENCES

Albanese, Catherine L. (2007). *A Republic of Mind and Spirit. A Cultural History of American Metaphysical Religion*. Yale University Press.

Eddy, Mary Baker. (1899). *Science and Health with Key to the Scriptures*. Joseph Armstrong.

Eddy, Mary Baker. (1900). *Miscellaneous Writings. 1883–1896*. Joseph Armstrong.

Hay, Louse. (1984). *You Can Heal Your Life*. Hay House.

Kunz, Dora. (1995). *Spiritual Healing*. Bear & Company.

Kunz, Dora and Delores Krieger. (2004). *The Spiritual Dimension of Therapeutic Touch*. Bear & Company.

## FURTHER READING


Alhstrom, Sydney E. (1972). *A Religious History of the American People*. Yale University Press.

Burger, Bruce. (1998). *Esoteric Anatomy. The Body as Consciousness*. North Atlantic Books.

Cox, Harvey. (1977). *Turning East. Why Americans Look to the Orient For Spirituality and What That Search Can Mean for the West*. Simon and Schuster.

Cranston, Sylvia. (1994). *HPB: The Extraordinary Life and Influence of Helena Blavatsky Founder of the Modern Theosophical Movement*. Jeremy Tarcher and Putnam Books.

Heelas, Paul. (1996). *The New Age Movement*. Blackwell.

Judith, Anodea. (2004). *Eastern Body, Western Mind. Psychology and the Chakra System as a Path to the Self*. Celestial Arts.

Karagulla, Shafica and Dora Van Gelder Kunz. (1989). *The Chakras and The Human Energy Fields*. Quest Books.

Krieger, Delores. (1979). *The Therapeutic Touch. How to Use Your Hands to Help and Heal*. Atria Books.

Krieger, Delores. (2021). *A Healer's Journey. The Heart of Therapeutic Touch*. Bear & Company.

Locklin, Reid B. (2005). *Spiritual But Not Religious? An Oar Stroke Closer To the Farther Shore*. Liturgical Press.

Macrae, Janet. (1988). *Therapeutic Touch. A Practical Guide*. Knopf.

Milmine, Georgine. (2016). *The Life of Mary Baker Eddy and the History of Christian Science*. Wentworth Press.

Owen, Alex. (2004). *The Place of Enchantment. British Occultism and the Culture of the Modern*. University of Chicago Press.

Partridge, Christopher. (2004). *The Re-Enchantment of the West. Volume 1*. T&T Clark International.

Pike, Sarah M. (2004). *New Age and Neopagan Religions in America*. Columbia University Press.

Shealy, C. Norman and Caroline M. Myss. (1988). *The Creation of Health: Merging Traditional Medicine with Intuitive Diagnosis*. Stillpoint.

Thiessen, Joel and Sarah Wilkins-Laflamme. (2020). *None of the Above: Non-Religious Identity in the US and Canada*. University of Regina Press.

Van Gelder, Kirsten and Frank Chelsey. (2015). *A Most Unusual Life Dora Van Gelder Kunz. Clairvoyant, Theosophist and Healer*. Quest Books.

Watts, Galen. (2022). *The Spiritual Turn. The Religion of the Heart and the Making of Romantic Liberal Modernity*. Oxford University Press.

Wuthnow, Robert. (1998). *After Heaven. Spirituality in America Since the 1950's*. University of California Press.

# Appendix 1

## Palliative Care: A New Model for Treating the Whole Person

Religion has been deeply intertwined in the care of the dying in all of the world's cultures. In western culture the Christian tradition has a long history of caring for those who are dying as part of the works of corporeal mercy stretching back to the beginnings of the tradition. However, when discussing hospices and palliative care in the contemporary period all roads lead to one woman.

Born into a wealthy British family, and a deeply religious person, the story of Cicely Saunders' idea of the modern hospice began when she was working as a nurse during World War II. Due to health challenges Saunders shifted to work as a social worker and then became a medical doctor. The watershed moment occurred in London in 1948 when she was caring for David Tasma a Polish-Jewish refugee who had survived the Warsaw ghetto and was dying of cancer alone in a foreign country.

In their long discussions on a busy and noisy ward, the idea of the modern hospice was born. The fact that the movement was born from a profound relationship would impact the whole conceptual framework of palliative care. Saunders oversaw the Jewish funeral of David Tasma embodying the idea that all palliative care should reflect the wishes of the person religious or non-religious.

As a result of this life-changing encounter Saunders felt that she now knew "what God wanted from me". From this point onwards she worked to bring a place into being that embodied their vision. Tasma left Saunders £500 in his will saying "I'll be a window in your house". Today this window exists in the front of the St Christopher's Hospice in Sydenham, UK.

Saunders was one of the few in the mid-20th century drawing attention to the gap in the healthcare system regarding chronic illness and end-of-life. Saunders (1961) wrote, "a society occupied with the pursuit of prosperity, security and tangible pleasures has no valid answers to the problems of suffering and death" (p. 53). Placing the needs of the patient at the centre, she set out to develop a model that combined the religious values of comfort and care with the biomedical approach to pain management.

Saunders drew on the long history of Christian healing in the development of a hospice model of care. Working with the Irish Sisters of Charity at St Joseph's Hospice in London Saunders noted how serene and content both the nurses and patients appeared to be. Many were able to maintain normal activities such as participating in family life, going to movies, or to the pub right up to the end. Saunders was particularly concerned with pain management at end of life and believed that being free of pain allowed the person to concentrate on relationships and living fully.

Developing her theories at a time when death denial was the norm Saunders was part of broader reevaluation regarding end-of-life care. The work of Elisabeth Kubler-Ross was part of this larger cultural shift that gained momentum in the 1970s. Saunders advocated for a radical new approach to end-of-life care combining attention to physical, social, emotional, and spiritual problems captured in her concept of "total pain".

Total pain referred to the many dimensions of human experience including emotional and spiritual struggles. For many at the end of life the pain may come in struggling with unresolved relationships and existential questions rather than simply physical symptoms. From this perspective this stage of life could be a time of reconciliation with family members and a period of self-reflection.

Working as she did with dying patients Saunders knew that each individual had a different experience depending on their age, family situation, and amount of support. The role of family and friends in support of the dying has always been central to Saunders' vision. Working with and supporting families both before and after death is an intrinsic part of the work of many hospices. This model of a strong community was meant to also support the nurses, doctors, and staff.

Saunders was active in spreading this new vision of palliative care and travelled extensively. On her trips to the US and Canada she developed an ongoing relationship with Florence Wald, then Dean of Nursing at Yale University and Balfour Mount, oncology surgeon and professor at McGill University, in Montreal. Both were pioneers in developing hospice care models in their respective countries. Saunders also lobbied for research and teaching of palliative care and made St Christopher's hospice a teaching institution.

A number of different versions of hospice and palliative care have emerged since St Christopher's was founded in 1967. Saunders always recognized that palliative care would adapt to the culture in which it was operating. They approaches include stand-alone hospices run with or without government funding, assisted in home care, and palliative care units as part of an existing hospital. Combinations of these approaches often occur with the patient kept at home as long as possible with support from nurses/social workers and then moved to the hospice if necessary.

The rapid progress of the international hospice and palliative care movement is no doubt related to the fact that it addresses many of the issues raised in this book. Emerging from a religious worldview it has created a form of health care that includes all aspects of the person including their mental, emotional and spiritual dimensions. Palliative care also draws on the support of the person's family, friends, and community.

Palliative medicine is now a sub-specialization for doctors and nurses in countries such as Britain, the US, and Canada. This model allows for the strengths of traditional religious approaches to death and dying to be combined with scientific approaches in a way that allows for a pain free and supported death alongside support for family and friends of the patient.

## *On the role of nurses*

...because they often are nearer to the patient than anyone else they may be faced with searching or ambiguous questions without warning. The nurse will have to say something. .... Patients, usually do not want our judgments or our explanations but rather our understanding, and often just our silent listening. They do not want to know what we think. They so want to know that we are interested in what they think. In no situation is it more true that "In quietness and in confidence shall be your strength".

(Saunders, 2006, p. 82)

## CASE STUDY: NIPISSING SERENITY HOSPICE NORTH BAY, ONTARIO, CANADA

In many ways Nipissing Serenity Hospice, which opened in North Bay, Ontario in 2020, is a typical example of a hospice. The building of the facility emerged directly from the community spearheaded by former nurse and lawyer, Mathilde Gravelle Bazinet. The City Council of North Bay then offered the founding board a site for building for the nominal fee of $1. The founding committee also secured a two million dollar grant from the provincial government.

The hospice was almost a decade in the making, and planning and fundraising resulted in its doors opening to the public in 2020. The stated aim of the hospice is to provide quality, compassionate, and holistic end-of-life palliative care. This requires a multidisciplinary team that includes physicians, nurses, personal support workers, social workers, palliative care volunteers, and multi-faith chaplaincy.

The hospice is also dedicated to supporting the families through the end-of-life process and after. It is bilingual (English/French) with a place on the board set aside for Indigenous representation. The hospice is built on the larger multicultural model and attempting to ensure each person receives culturally and religiously congruent care.

Nipissing Serenity Hospice is very much of its place and reflects its environment leaning in to the beauty of the northern Canadian setting. The hospice is adjacent to a conservation area with a stream running past and the building is oriented so patients can sit either outside or inside a screened in the porch area. The building also includes a Sacred Room meant for reflection, prayer, or meditation.

The support of the larger community in the form of donations and volunteers' hours is ongoing and reflects the larger landscape of palliative care in Ontario. The Compassionate Care Act passed unanimously in provincial parliament in 2020. This unprecedented show of political unity demonstrates how far Saunders' vision has come to fruition. Increasingly, people around the world now recognize the need for a new model for end-of-life care shaped by the ideals of compassion and support.

## MATHILDE GRAVELLE BAZINET RN, LLD, FOUNDER, NIPISSING SERENITY HOSPICE, RN, JD, MEMBER OF THE ORDER OF CANADA

Mathilde Gravelle Bazinet's commitment to palliative and hospice care comes both from her many years of nursing and also experiences in her personal life. Early in her nursing career she was appalled to find that those who were dying were often taken to a utility room to be apart from the regular patients and that they often died alone. The case of a young boy dying in her arms, without his parents present, set Bazinet on the path to ensuring that no one was left alone at the end of their life.

In contrast to what she had experienced as a nurse, Bazinet's brother died in a hospice setting and the atmosphere was the complete opposite where both the patient and family were supported. Her nephews, who had been estranged, were also able to be present and reconcile and their father was able to pass peacefully.

Having seen what was possible Bazinet and set out on her path to ensuring these services were available within her own community. Noting the many challenges she and the team faced Bazinet recalls that when she was feeling down hearted her mother would appear in her dreams saying, "you have to finish the job you started".

Bazinet is very open about the fact that her Catholic faith is what has inspired both her nursing vocation and her drive to make palliative care available to all. She is inspired by the New Testament instruction, "*Ce que tu fais aux plus petits d'entre les miens, c'est à moi même que tu le fais*". ("What you do for the least, you do for me".)

## VIVIAN PAPAIZ FOUNDING CHAIR OF THE BOARD, NIPISSING SERENITY HOSPICE

Vivian Papaiz, RN, PhD, began her career as an emergency room nurse. After the birth of her children, she moved into community nursing and it was there she realized that she needed different skills for dealing with patients at the end of life. Papaiz began to take courses in palliative care where she learned about complex pain management and how to work with the dying and their families. As she puts it this work with patients and their families, "is when I really understood what nursing is really about".

Papaiz went on to take up leadership roles in the hospice and palliative care community. Serving as Chair of Hospice and Palliative Care Ontario (HPCO) 2019–2021 she is currently President of the Canadian Hospice and Palliative Care Association (CHPCA). Papaiz is committed to ensuring that people are cared for allowing for comfort and dignity at the end-of-life. This concern which she refers to as sacred work includes the care and support of families.

According to Papaiz working with people at end of life means, "We are often the closest to the people in their most vulnerable time". She believes that the nursing curriculum would benefit from more direct engagement with the issues around hospice, palliative care, and how to handle conversations with patients and their families. For Papaiz an expanded curriculum would bring in the art as well as technique of nursing as the human side is the "quintessential form of care".

## GIL PHARAND, EXECUTIVE DIRECTOR NIPISSING SERENITY HOSPICE

Gil Pharand began his career working in the non-profit sector out of a desire to give back to the community and to "do some good in the world". After the death of his mother from cancer he was determined to work in the area of cancer research and end of life. He said that he would have ensured that his mother had gone to a hospice, "if I knew then what I know now".

Pharand is determined that all in his community have access to hospice care. He notes that Nipissing Serenity Hospice is committed to supporting the cultural and spiritual needs of residents alongside medical care. The facility offers a Sacred Room and installed a system that allows for smudging and maintains contact with religious and spiritual caregivers as desired. "We don't pretend to experts on all traditions but we work to ensure that we connect patients to those in the community who are".

Pharand notes that there is still a stigma around death and dying and that generally people don't have conversations about it until they have to. He sees the hospice as playing a vital role, because they are cost effective, free up hospital beds, and because they can support people in grief and bereavement. Noting that the building and its surrounding are beautiful he emphasizes, "the building is very important but it's not about the building it is about the people".

## REFERENCES

Kubler-Ross, Elisabeth. (1973). *On Death and Dying*. Routledge.

Saunders, Cicely. (2006). *Cicely Saunders: Selected Writings 1958–2004*. Oxford University Press.

Wood, Joe and Cicely Saunders. (2022). 'Total Pain' and Emotional Evidence at the End of Life. *Medical Humanities*, 48 (4), 411–20.

## FURTHER READING

Clark, David. (2016). *To Comfort Always: A History of Palliative Medicine Since the Nineteenth Century*. Oxford University Press.

Du Boulay, Shirley. (1984). *Cicely Saunders: founder of the modern hospice movement*. Hodder and Stoughton.

Floriano, Carol Milardo. (1999). The Spiritual Side of Pain. Hospice Caregivers Help a Suffering Patient Make Peace With His Religions. *American Journal of Nursing*, 99 (5).

Nagel, Allen. (1990). Hospice to Hospital in the Near East: An Instance of Continuity and Change in Late Antiquity. *BHM*, 64, 446–62.

## INTERNET RESOURCES

Hospice and Palliative Care Ontario (HPCO): https://www.hpco.ca/
Nipissing Serenity Hospice: https://nipissingserenityhospice.ca/
St Christopher's Hospice: https://www.stchristophers.org.uk/

# Appendix 2

## Therapeutic Environments: Sacred Space as Healing Space

When considering the many connections between religion and health and healing the creation of a sacred space is a vital and often overlooked part of the larger process of healing. Sacred sites vary from the most personal, individual, family altars to destinations that attract millions of visitors each year.

Whether large or small these spaces share the same logic of establishing a refuge set aside for religious practice, prayer, ritual, and ceremony. These spaces open up a zone for individuals or groups to engage in healing both in established modes and rituals but also ways that suit them best and fit their needs.

A common way to access sacred space is by making a trip to a religious place. Pilgrimage is based on the idea that certain places on the earth are closer to the divine. Going on a pilgrimage to seek healing, either mental or physical, is a common religious practice that is only gaining in popularity. Pilgrimage sites may have religious buildings dedicated to particular concerns and a common one is heath and healing. These areas in turn act as dense cultural nodes featuring sacred architecture, rituals, objects and are believed to hold particular religious power.

### HISTORICAL SITES OF HEALING: THE ASCLEPION

The Asclepion of the ancient Greek world offer a comprehensive model of a therapeutic environment. Because of this they continue to influence ideas about health and healing into the present inspiring the idea of the spa as well as holistic forms of health. Typically located in sites of natural beauty and away from urban centres they were sites of pilgrimage for those seeking health and healing.

These sites included the many dimensions of healing: nature as cure, mythology, drama, ritual and ceremony, diet, exercise, aesthetics, art, and ritual. While these are generally separated out into fragments in the contemporary world, from a spiritual standpoint they functioned most effectively in concert. All of these were held within a larger religious worldview that saw healing as coming from a divine source.

The fact that a theatre (*odeion*) was a feature of all the major Asclepions demonstrates the central role played by ritual and drama in these settings. This points to the fact that theatre was not simply for entertainment or diversion in the world of ancient Greece but was dedicated to the Gods and Goddesses.

One of the key elements as understood by philosophers like Aristotle was that the performance of tragedies, "effecting through pity and fear the purification (katharsis) of such emotions" (xxxvi).

The Asclepion was believed to be a site where the sacred was concentrated and so healing would be more likely to take place. The central ritual was the practice of dream incubation (see Appendix 3). These rituals were meant to facilitate healing through dreams of the God of Healing Asclepius or through other healing images.

## LOURDES AS SITE OF HEALING

Lourdes is a pilgrimage destination in southern France that attracts over five million visitors of a year. The site is dedicated to healing and is an example of grassroots and institutional religion coming together. The shrine originated from a vision of the Virgin Mary received by a French peasant girl named Bernadette Soubrious (1843–1879).

According to her description of her visions the Virgin Mary told her to tell the priests to build a chapel on the spot and that people should come for prayer and penitence and to drink and bathe in the spring. Her vision was greeted with skepticism but people began to arrive and a small shrine was set up to the Virgin Mary.

The Vatican officially accepted the shrine as a holy site in 1862 and a church was built. While many travel to Lourdes on their own larger pilgrimage groups are common. A special White Train carries the sick from Paris to Lourdes every year on August 15, the Feast Day of the Assumption of the Virgin as part of the French National Pilgrimage.

This train carries *les grande maladies* cases that science has declared itself powerless to relieve. On the day of departure, at Austerlitz station in Paris rows of stretchers are lined up and they are blessed by the Cardinal Archbishop of Paris.

Volunteers or family accompany the sick on this journey. For these volunteers it is a form of charitable service and a way to renew their religious commitment. A special order called the Hospitallers aid the pilgrims by praying continuously for the sick, helping them to dress, helping them on and off buses and wheeling them to the grotto.

Pilgrims to Lourdes participate in a variety of rituals but the central one is a bath in one of the pools filled with the water from the spring that Saint Bernadette uncovered. Each patient/pilgrim is immersed in the water and often water from the spring is taken back home with the pilgrim.

Many cures have been associated with the shrine but as David Kinsley (1996) notes the majority of pilgrims to Lourdes do not experience a dramatic physical healing of their illness. And this is understood by pilgrims who say that the soul can be cured without a healing of the physical body. One man who went hoping for a cure for paralysis said he became increasingly interested in the people around him and stated:

> I still prayed for my cure, but on the second day I became ashamed of myself .... I started praying for the blind man and the consumptive and since that moment I have felt that I should think of others and not myself.
>
> *(p. 116)*

This man went on to work as a volunteer nurse at Lourdes every year. Going to Lourdes allowed him to reframe his experience. As a result, he stated that while his physical situation remained the same, "I have found contentment and my soul is cured" (ibid.).

The fact that Lourdes is a space where those who are ill or disabled are often in the majority is a potent aspect of the power of the site. Kinsley notes that the sick also pray for the well at Lourdes because from a religious perspective illness is not only physical. These prayers recognize that mental anguish can be as incapacitating and painful as any illness. These prayers also impress upon the physically well that all are in need of some kind of healing.

> The atmosphere is charged with emotions and pilgrims are assisted and prepared for their bath with efficiency, respect and dignity. As they enter the other side of the curtain, their robe is changed for a bathing sheet and then they stand before our Lady and silently pray for their intentions. When they finish their silent prayer, they make the sign of the cross before being led down the bath area and the pilgrim is submerged into the water backwards with their heads, necks and backs being supported by the volunteer helpers like myself. Words cannot begin to express how powerful this experience is but there is an undeniable connection with Our Lady that touches my very spirit and with every bath encounter I found that each individual pilgrim brings a unique and special experience.
>
> —Angela McCulloch, *My Experience of Working in the Baths at Lourdes as a Volunteer*.

## REFERENCES

Kinsley, David. (1996). *Health, Healing and Religion. A Cross-Cultural Perspective*. Prentice Hall.

McCulloch, Angela, *My Experience of Working in the Baths at Lourdes as a Volunteer*, Oblate News, https://oblates.ie/lourdes-volunteer/

## FURTHER READING

Agnew, Michael. (2015). Spiritually I'm Always at Lourdes. Perceptions of Home and Away Among Serial Pilgrims. *Studies in Religion*, 44 (4), 516–35.

Aristotle. (1996). *Poetics*. Translated by Malcolm Health. Penguin Books.

Harris, Ruth. (1999). *Lourdes. Body and Spirit in the Secular Age*. Penguin Books.

Hartigan, Karelisa V. (2009). *Performance and Cure. Drama and Healing in Ancient Greece and Contemporary America*. Duckworth.

Ohnuki-Tierney, Emiko. (1989). Healthcare in Contemporary Japanese Religions. *Healing and Restoring: Health and Medicine in the World's Religious Tradition*. Lawrence E. Sullivan (Ed.). Macmillian Publishing.

Wright, Stephen G. and Jean Sayre-Adams. (2000). *Sacred Space, Right Relationship and Spirituality in Healthcare*. Churchill Livingstone.

# Appendix 3

## Working With Healing Dreams: Ancient and Contemporary Techniques

The general secular attitude towards dreams can be summed up in Scrooge's reaction to his shattering night visions which he attributes to indigestion. Despite this typical attitude many, if not most, people have had dreams that woke them in the night or have recurred throughout their lives. The early pioneers of psychology Sigmund Freud and Carl Jung both paid particular attention to dreams in their practices of psychology. But in the western world respect for this universal phenomenon is at an all-time low. As Mittermaier (2010), a scholar who researches Muslim approaches to dreams puts it in the western world we live in "undreamy times" (p. 1).

The world's religious traditions have another story to tell about dreams. Both the Hebrew and Christian Bibles contain descriptions of dreams, perhaps the most famous being Daniel's role as dream interpreter for the Egyptian pharaoh. In the Islamic tradition it is believed that the Qu'ran was received by the Prophet Muhammed in a dream state and dreams have retained their status as vital ways that the divine communicates with human beings.

Robert Moss states that for the Haudesaosnee (Iroquois) those who do not dream, who do not remember and value their dreams, are at risk for losing touch with their deepest dimensions of their life. The realms of dream and vision, in many of the world's traditions are a place where vital new ideas and practices can enter into a culture and where the sacred can meet the mundane world.

Ian Barasch (2000) notes the numerous words for different kinds of dreams in New Testament Greek (p. 19). Barasch himself was brought to working on the topic of dreams by his own overwhelmingly powerful dreams and consequent journey through a life-threatening illness. After recovering he set out on a journey to examine healing dreams around the world.

All across the world popular books on dreams and dream interpretation continue to have a wide audience. In Wanda Burch's *She Who Dreams: A Journey Into Healing Through Dreamwork* (2003) she recounts her childhood in an Irish American family that took dreams seriously. When Burch was diagnosed with breast cancer, she immediately began working with dream imagery alongside medical treatment. Burch has gone on to teach workshops on dreams and healing.

Many cultures, and subcultures, continue to take dreams seriously. Professional and religiously based dream interpreters remain ubiquitous throughout the Muslim world. Many psychologists also examine and use the information and images provided by dreams in their work. The idea that dreams have vital messages to offer regarding mental and physical healing stretches from antiquity into the present.

## THE ASCLEPIA: DREAM INCUBATION AND HEALING IN ANCIENT GREECE

At its zenith it is estimated there were 200 Ascleipia in the world of ancient Greece stretching across what is now Greece, Turkey, and Italy. Archaeological digs reveal vast complexes set in beautiful natural surroundings. These spaces epitomized the Greek approach to healing with its emphasis on the unity of mind, body, and spirit and the healing power of nature.

These complexes included shrines dedicated to the gods and goddesses, a theatre, a library, and sacred well. Within the enclosure visitors were ushered into the sacred space through a long corridor. Entering into the sacred complex the pilgrim was now cut off from his or her normal life for a period of time.

The preliminary treatment when entering into the Asclepions was *katharsis*, or purification. It consisted of a series of prayers, cleansing baths, and purgations, accompanied by a cleansing diet, which lasted several days. Then the supplicant was admitted into the sanctuary proper to participate in the Asclepian rites.

After the purification process the supplicant entered the Abaton or dream incubation chamber for one or more nights, to receive a healing dream from Asclepius. If the patient/pilgrim was lucky, he or she would receive a personal visitation from the Divine Physician himself, who would either heal the person directly in the dream state, or offer a prescription for what to do to cure his or her illness. The physician/priests at the Asclepions were also dream interpreters who would divine the treatment to be followed from the patient's account of their healing dream.

## *Gitte Bechsgaard, Registered Therapist.*

### Using Dreams in Therapy: "Dreams Never Lie"

Gitte Bechsgaard uses dreams as the basis of her psychological work in 25% of cases and in 50% use dreams alongside counseling. Bechsgaard sees dreams as being the bridge between psychological and spiritual work. Her biggest influences in relation to dream therapy are Carl Jung and her mentors Anna Binswanger, Jim Healy, and Adam Crabtree during her training at the Centre for Training in Psychotherapy (CTP) in Toronto.

As part of her training to become a psychotherapist, Bechsgaard did many hours of her own dream analysis, study, and group dream work. She sees dreams as the one of the primary routes to the Self and believes that they offer vital, "resources for healing". This can include either mental, emotional, or physical healing or all three.

### How Dreams May Be Used in a Session

When working with a dream Bechsgaard asks the clients to begin to write down their dreams. She may ask them to give the dream a title. When in session the person is asked to tell it to her twice. In this way working with the dream becomes, "a kind of meditative, contemplative process". Then she asks what speaks to them in the dream—what stands out, what is the emotional tone of the dream. The images can act as "a kind of barometer" of the overall situation.

Bechsgaard is quick to note that any interpretation has to resonate with the dreamer. It is not a mechanical process or attempt to "crack the code" and will vary from person to person and dream to dream requiring attunement and deep listening on the part of the therapist. The setting of the dream will generally point to the area of life that it is speaking to, i.e. a dream set in an office will often point to work-related issues.

Images of vehicles and certain animal imagery may speak to the overall condition of the psyche and body. "An image of a wounded animal is one that has to be taken seriously", says Bechsgaard. This image is often a warning dream speaking to a situation in which the person's well-being is being put into jeopardy. Following up on a dream of this sort may include visiting a doctor or attending to one's health in concrete ways such as taking more time for oneself or scheduling a treatment such as massage.

Bechsgaard notes that, along with more archetypal meanings, each person can develop their own symbolic vocabulary. Certain symbols are more universal such as spiders and spider's webs often referring to a mother complex or jewels and jewellery pointing to what is most precious in life. However, some symbols will be idiosyncratic based on the person's life experiences.

When working with healing dreams Bechsgaard has found that personal healing symbols are the most effective. One client used an image that emerged from a dream of sitting in the sunshine in a field a poppies to support her as she went through chemotherapy. These images can be worked with in meditation or in visualizations.

According to Bechsgaard dreams have their own intelligence and will often point towards what is needed to resolve or improve a given situation. Taking some kind of action is often part of the practice. This could include booking an appointment for tests or performing a ritual.

Dreams used in this way foster attention to the inner life and self-awareness. It is typical for clients to have presenting dreams when they enter into therapy that lay out what needs to be worked on in the course of the therapy.

The dreams, according to Bechsgaard are readily available sources of wisdom related to all aspects of life and are so valuable because, "dreams never lie".

## REFERENCES

Barasch, Marc Ian. (2000). *Healing Dreams*. Riverhead Books.

Bechsgaard, Gitte. Interview with author, May 2023. February 2024.

Burch, Wanda. (2010). *She Who Dreams. A Journey Into Healing Through Dreamwork*. New World Library.

Mittermaier, Amira. (2010). *Dreams That Matter: Egyptian Landscapes of the Imagination*. University of California Press.

Moss, Robert. (2009). *The Secret History of Dreaming*. World Library.

## FURTHER READING

Flannery-Dailey, Frances. (2004). *Dreamers, Scribes and Priests. Jewish Dreams in the Hellenic and Roman Era*. Leiden: Brill.

Holloway, Gillian. (2006). *The Complete Dream Book. Discover What Your Dreams Reveal About You and Your Life*. sourcebooks.

Meier, C. A. (1989). *Healing Dreams and Ritual. Ancient Incubation and Modern Psychiatry*. Einsedeln, Switzerland: Daimon-Verlag.

Renberg, Gil H. (2017). *Where Dreams May Come. Incubation Sanctuaries in the Greco-Roman World*. Leiden: Brill.

Sobel, Mechal. (2002). *Teach Me Dreams. The Search for Self in the Revolutionary Era*. Princeton University Press.

# Index

Note: Locators in ***italic-bold*** indicate boxes.

Kolibri 360 GmbH
Ferdinand-Jühlke-Straße 7
99095 Erfurt, Deutschland
produktsicherheit@kolibri360.de